ITBS
Success Strategies
Level 9 Grade 3

DEAR FUTURE EXAM SUCCESS STORY

First of all, **THANK YOU** for purchasing Mometrix study materials!

Second, congratulations! You are one of the few determined test-takers who are committed to doing whatever it takes to excel on your exam. **You have come to the right place.** We developed these study materials with one goal in mind: to deliver you the information you need in a format that's concise and easy to use.

In addition to optimizing your guide for the content of the test, we've outlined our recommended steps for breaking down the preparation process into small, attainable goals so you can make sure you stay on track.

We've also analyzed the entire test-taking process, identifying the most common pitfalls and showing how you can overcome them and be ready for any curveball the test throws you.

Standardized testing is one of the biggest obstacles on your road to success, which only increases the importance of doing well in the high-pressure, high-stakes environment of test day. Your results on this test could have a significant impact on your future, and this guide provides the information and practical advice to help you achieve your full potential on test day.

Your success is our success

We would love to hear from you! If you would like to share the story of your exam success or if you have any questions or comments in regard to our products, please contact us at **800-673-8175** or **support@mometrix.com**.

Thanks again for your business and we wish you continued success!

Sincerely,
The Mometrix Test Preparation Team

TABLE OF CONTENTS

Introduction

Thank you for purchasing this resource! You have made the choice to prepare yourself for a test that could have a huge impact on your future, and this guide is designed to help you be fully ready for test day. Obviously, it's important to have a solid understanding of the test material, but you also need to be prepared for the unique environment and stressors of the test, so that you can perform to the best of your abilities.

For this purpose, the first section that appears in this guide is the **Success Strategies**. We've devoted countless hours to meticulously researching what works and what doesn't, and we've boiled down our findings to the five most impactful steps you can take to improve your performance on the test. We start at the beginning with study planning and move through the preparation process, all the way to the testing strategies that will help you get the most out of what you know when you're finally sitting in front of the test.

We recommend that you start preparing for your test as far in advance as possible. However, if you've bought this guide as a last-minute study resource and only have a few days before your test, we recommend that you skip over the first two Success Strategies since they address a long-term study plan.

If you struggle with **test anxiety**, we strongly encourage you to check out our recommendations for how you can overcome it. Test anxiety is a formidable foe, but it can be beaten, and we want to make sure you have the tools you need to defeat it.

1

Strategy #1 – Plan Big, Study Small

There's a lot riding on your performance. If you want to ace this test, you're going to need to keep your skills sharp and the material fresh in your mind. You need a plan that lets you review everything you need to know while still fitting in your schedule. We'll break this strategy down into three categories.

Information Organization

Start with the information you already have: the official test outline. From this, you can make a complete list of all the concepts you need to cover before the test. Organize these concepts into groups that can be studied together, and create a list of any related vocabulary you need to learn so you can brush up on any difficult terms. You'll want to keep this vocabulary list handy once you actually start studying since you may need to add to it along the way.

Time Management

Once you have your set of study concepts, decide how to spread them out over the time you have left before the test. Break your study plan into small, clear goals so you have a manageable task for each day and know exactly what you're doing. Then just focus on one small step at a time. When you manage your time this way, you don't need to spend hours at a time studying. Studying a small block of content for a short period each day helps you retain information better and avoid stressing over how much you have left to do. You can relax knowing that you have a plan to cover everything in time. In order for this strategy to be effective though, you have to start studying early and stick to your schedule. Avoid the exhaustion and futility that comes from last-minute cramming!

Study Environment

The environment you study in has a big impact on your learning. Studying in a coffee shop, while probably more enjoyable, is not likely to be as fruitful as studying in a quiet room. It's important to keep distractions to a minimum. You're only planning to study for a short block of time, so make the most of it. Don't pause to check your phone or get up to find a snack. It's also important to **avoid multitasking**. Research has consistently shown that multitasking will make your studying dramatically less effective. Your study area should also be comfortable and well-lit so you don't have the distraction of straining your eyes or sitting on an uncomfortable chair.

 The time of day you study is also important. You want to be rested and alert. Don't wait until just before bedtime. Study when you'll be most likely to comprehend and remember. Even better, if you know what time of day your test will be, set that time aside for study. That way your brain will be used to working on that subject at that specific time and you'll have a better chance of recalling information.

Finally, it can be helpful to team up with others who are studying for the same test. Your actual studying should be done in as isolated an environment as possible, but the work of organizing the information and setting up the study plan can be divided up. In between study sessions, you can discuss with your teammates the concepts that you're all studying and quiz each other on the details. Just be sure that your teammates are as serious about the test as you are. If you find that your study time is being replaced with social time, you might need to find a new team.

Strategy #2 – Make Your Studying Count

You're devoting a lot of time and effort to preparing for this test, so you want to be absolutely certain it will pay off. This means doing more than just reading the content and hoping you can remember it on test day. It's important to make every minute of study count. There are two main areas you can focus on to make your studying count.

Retention

It doesn't matter how much time you study if you can't remember the material. You need to make sure you are retaining the concepts. To check your retention of the information you're learning, try recalling it at later times with minimal prompting. Try carrying around flashcards and glance at one or two from time to time or ask a friend who's also studying for the test to quiz you.

To enhance your retention, look for ways to put the information into practice so that you can apply it rather than simply recalling it. If you're using the information in practical ways, it will be much easier to remember. Similarly, it helps to solidify a concept in your mind if you're not only reading it to yourself but also explaining it to someone else. Ask a friend to let you teach them about a concept you're a little shaky on (or speak aloud to an imaginary audience if necessary). As you try to summarize, define, give examples, and answer your friend's questions, you'll understand the concepts better and they will stay with you longer. Finally, step back for a big picture view and ask yourself how each piece of information fits with the whole subject. When you link the different concepts together and see them working together as a whole, it's easier to remember the individual components.

Finally, practice showing your work on any multi-step problems, even if you're just studying. Writing out each step you take to solve a problem will help solidify the process in your mind, and you'll be more likely to remember it during the test.

Modality

Modality simply refers to the means or method by which you study. Choosing a study modality that fits your own individual learning style is crucial. No two people learn best in exactly the same way, so it's important to know your strengths and use them to your advantage.

For example, if you learn best by visualization, focus on visualizing a concept in your mind and draw an image or a diagram. Try color-coding your notes, illustrating them, or creating symbols that will trigger your mind to recall a learned concept. If you learn best by hearing or discussing information, find a study partner who learns the same way or read aloud to yourself. Think about how to put the information in your own words. Imagine that you are giving a lecture on the topic and record yourself so you can listen to it later.

For any learning style, flashcards can be helpful. Organize the information so you can take advantage of spare moments to review. Underline key words or phrases. Use different colors for different categories. Mnemonic devices (such as creating a short list in which every item starts with the same letter) can also help with retention. Find what works best for you and use it to store the information in your mind most effectively and easily.

3

Strategy #3 – Practice the Right Way

Your success on test day depends not only on how many hours you put into preparing, but also on whether you prepared the right way. It's good to check along the way to see if your studying is paying off. One of the most effective ways to do this is by taking practice tests to evaluate your progress. Practice tests are useful because they show exactly where you need to improve. Every time you take a practice test, pay special attention to these three groups of questions:

- The questions you got wrong
- The questions you had to guess on, even if you guessed right
- The questions you found difficult or slow to work through

This will show you exactly what your weak areas are, and where you need to devote more study time. Ask yourself why each of these questions gave you trouble. Was it because you didn't understand the material? Was it because you didn't remember the vocabulary? Do you need more repetitions on this type of question to build speed and confidence? Dig into those questions and figure out how you can strengthen your weak areas as you go back to review the material.

 Additionally, many practice tests have a section explaining the answer choices. It can be tempting to read the explanation and think that you now have a good understanding of the concept. However, an explanation likely only covers part of the question's broader context. Even if the explanation makes perfect sense, **go back and investigate** every concept related to the question until you're positive you have a thorough understanding.

As you go along, keep in mind that the practice test is just that: practice. Memorizing these questions and answers will not be very helpful on the actual test because it is unlikely to have any of the same exact questions. If you only know the right answers to the sample questions, you won't be prepared for the real thing. **Study the concepts** until you understand them fully, and then you'll be able to answer any question that shows up on the test.

It's important to wait on the practice tests until you're ready. If you take a test on your first day of study, you may be overwhelmed by the amount of material covered and how much you need to learn. Work up to it gradually.

On test day, you'll need to be prepared for answering questions, managing your time, and using the test-taking strategies you've learned. It's a lot to balance, like a mental marathon that will have a big impact on your future. Like training for a marathon, you'll need to start slowly and work your way up. When test day arrives, you'll be ready.

Start with the strategies you've read in the first two Success Strategies—plan your course and study in the way that works best for you. If you have time, consider using multiple study resources to get different approaches to the same concepts. It can be helpful to see difficult concepts from more than one angle. Then find a good source for practice tests. Many times, the test website will suggest potential study resources or provide sample tests.

Practice Test Strategy

If you're able to find at least three practice tests, we recommend this strategy:

UNTIMED AND OPEN-BOOK PRACTICE

Take the first test with no time constraints and with your notes and study guide handy. Take your time and focus on applying the strategies you've learned.

TIMED AND OPEN-BOOK PRACTICE

Take the second practice test open-book as well, but set a timer and practice pacing yourself to finish in time.

TIMED AND CLOSED-BOOK PRACTICE

Take any other practice tests as if it were test day. Set a timer and put away your study materials. Sit at a table or desk in a quiet room, imagine yourself at the testing center, and answer questions as quickly and accurately as possible.

Keep repeating timed and closed-book tests on a regular basis until you run out of practice tests or it's time for the actual test. Your mind will be ready for the schedule and stress of test day, and you'll be able to focus on recalling the material you've learned.

Strategy #4 – Pace Yourself

Once you're fully prepared for the material on the test, your biggest challenge on test day will be managing your time. Just knowing that the clock is ticking can make you panic even if you have plenty of time left. Work on pacing yourself so you can build confidence against the time constraints of the exam. Pacing is a difficult skill to master, especially in a high-pressure environment, so **practice is vital**.

Set time expectations for your pace based on how much time is available. For example, if a section has 60 questions and the time limit is 30 minutes, you know you have to average 30 seconds or less per question in order to answer them all. Although 30 seconds is the hard limit, set 25 seconds per question as your goal, so you reserve extra time to spend on harder questions. When you budget extra time for the harder questions, you no longer have any reason to stress when those questions take longer to answer.

Don't let this time expectation distract you from working through the test at a calm, steady pace, but keep it in mind so you don't spend too much time on any one question. Recognize that taking extra time on one question you don't understand may keep you from answering two that you do understand later in the test. If your time limit for a question is up and you're still not sure of the answer, mark it and move on, and come back to it later if the time and the test format allow. If the testing format doesn't allow you to return to earlier questions, just make an educated guess; then put it out of your mind and move on.

On the easier questions, be careful not to rush. It may seem wise to hurry through them so you have more time for the challenging ones, but it's not worth missing one if you know the concept and just didn't take the time to read the question fully. Work efficiently but make sure you understand the question and have looked at all of the answer choices, since more than one may seem right at first.

Even if you're paying attention to the time, you may find yourself a little behind at some point. You should speed up to get back on track, but do so wisely. Don't panic; just take a few seconds less on each question until you're caught up. Don't guess without thinking, but do look through the answer choices and eliminate any you know are wrong. If you can get down to two choices, it is often worthwhile to guess from those. Once you've chosen an answer, move on and don't dwell on any that you skipped or had to hurry through. If a question was taking too long, chances are it was one of the harder ones, so you weren't as likely to get it right anyway.

On the other hand, if you find yourself getting ahead of schedule, it may be beneficial to slow down a little. The more quickly you work, the more likely you are to make a careless mistake that will affect your score. You've budgeted time for each question, so don't be afraid to spend that time. Practice an efficient but careful pace to get the most out of the time you have.

Test-Taking Strategies

This section contains a list of test-taking strategies that you may find helpful as you work through the test. By taking what you know and applying logical thought, you can maximize your chances of answering any question correctly!

It is very important to realize that every question is different and every person is different: no single strategy will work on every question, and no single strategy will work for every person. That's why we've included all of them here, so you can try them out and determine which ones work best for different types of questions and which ones work best for you.

Question Strategies

ⓥ READ CAREFULLY

Read the question and the answer choices carefully. Don't miss the question because you misread the terms. You have plenty of time to read each question thoroughly and make sure you understand what is being asked. Yet a happy medium must be attained, so don't waste too much time. You must read carefully and efficiently.

ⓥ CONTEXTUAL CLUES

Look for contextual clues. If the question includes a word you are not familiar with, look at the immediate context for some indication of what the word might mean. Contextual clues can often give you all the information you need to decipher the meaning of an unfamiliar word. Even if you can't determine the meaning, you may be able to narrow down the possibilities enough to make a solid guess at the answer to the question.

ⓥ PREFIXES

If you're having trouble with a word in the question or answer choices, try dissecting it. Take advantage of every clue that the word might include. Prefixes can be a huge help. Usually, they allow you to determine a basic meaning. *Pre-* means before, *post-* means after, *pro-* is positive, *de-* is negative. From prefixes, you can get an idea of the general meaning of the word and try to put it into context.

ⓥ HEDGE WORDS

Watch out for critical hedge words, such as *likely, may, can, sometimes, often, almost, mostly, usually, generally, rarely,* and *sometimes.* Question writers insert these hedge phrases to cover every possibility. Often an answer choice will be wrong simply because it leaves no room for exception. Be on guard for answer choices that have definitive words such as *exactly* and *always.*

ⓥ SWITCHBACK WORDS

Stay alert for *switchbacks.* These are the words and phrases frequently used to alert you to shifts in thought. The most common switchback words are *but, although,* and *however.* Others include *nevertheless, on the other hand, even though, while, in spite of, despite,* and *regardless of.* Switchback words are important to catch because they can change the direction of the question or an answer choice.

7

⊘ FACE VALUE

When in doubt, use common sense. Accept the situation in the problem at face value. Don't read too much into it. These problems will not require you to make wild assumptions. If you have to go beyond creativity and warp time or space in order to have an answer choice fit the question, then you should move on and consider the other answer choices. These are normal problems rooted in reality. The applicable relationship or explanation may not be readily apparent, but it is there for you to figure out. Use your common sense to interpret anything that isn't clear.

Answer Choice Strategies

⊘ ANSWER SELECTION

The most thorough way to pick an answer choice is to identify and eliminate wrong answers until only one is left, then confirm it is the correct answer. Sometimes an answer choice may immediately seem right, but be careful. The test writers will usually put more than one reasonable answer choice on each question, so take a second to read all of them and make sure that the other choices are not equally obvious. As long as you have time left, it is better to read every answer choice than to pick the first one that looks right without checking the others.

⊘ ANSWER CHOICE FAMILIES

An answer choice family consists of two (in rare cases, three) answer choices that are very similar in construction and cannot all be true at the same time. If you see two answer choices that are direct opposites or parallels, one of them is usually the correct answer. For instance, if one answer choice says that quantity *x* increases and another either says that quantity *x* decreases (opposite) or says that quantity *y* increases (parallel), then those answer choices would fall into the same family. An answer choice that doesn't match the construction of the answer choice family is more likely to be incorrect. Most questions will not have answer choice families, but when they do appear, you should be prepared to recognize them.

⊘ ELIMINATE ANSWERS

Eliminate answer choices as soon as you realize they are wrong, but make sure you consider all possibilities. If you are eliminating answer choices and realize that the last one you are left with is also wrong, don't panic. Start over and consider each choice again. There may be something you missed the first time that you will realize on the second pass.

⊘ AVOID FACT TRAPS

Don't be distracted by an answer choice that is factually true but doesn't answer the question. You are looking for the choice that answers the question. Stay focused on what the question is asking for so you don't accidentally pick an answer that is true but incorrect. Always go back to the question and make sure the answer choice you've selected actually answers the question and is not merely a true statement.

⊘ EXTREME STATEMENTS

In general, you should avoid answers that put forth extreme actions as standard practice or proclaim controversial ideas as established fact. An answer choice that states the "process should be used in certain situations, if..." is much more likely to be correct than one that states the "process should be discontinued completely." The first is a calm rational statement and doesn't even make a definitive, uncompromising stance, using a hedge word *if* to provide wiggle room, whereas the second choice is far more extreme.

8

⌀ BENCHMARK

As you read through the answer choices and you come across one that seems to answer the question well, mentally select that answer choice. This is not your final answer, but it's the one that will help you evaluate the other answer choices. The one that you selected is your benchmark or standard for judging each of the other answer choices. Every other answer choice must be compared to your benchmark. That choice is correct until proven otherwise by another answer choice beating it. If you find a better answer, then that one becomes your new benchmark. Once you've decided that no other choice answers the question as well as your benchmark, you have your final answer.

⌀ PREDICT THE ANSWER

Before you even start looking at the answer choices, it is often best to try to predict the answer. When you come up with the answer on your own, it is easier to avoid distractions and traps because you will know exactly what to look for. The right answer choice is unlikely to be word-for-word what you came up with, but it should be a close match. Even if you are confident that you have the right answer, you should still take the time to read each option before moving on.

General Strategies

⌀ TOUGH QUESTIONS

If you are stumped on a problem or it appears too hard or too difficult, don't waste time. Move on! Remember though, if you can quickly check for obviously incorrect answer choices, your chances of guessing correctly are greatly improved. Before you completely give up, at least try to knock out a couple of possible answers. Eliminate what you can and then guess at the remaining answer choices before moving on.

⌀ CHECK YOUR WORK

Since you will probably not know every term listed and the answer to every question, it is important that you get credit for the ones that you do know. Don't miss any questions through careless mistakes. If at all possible, try to take a second to look back over your answer selection and make sure you've selected the correct answer choice and haven't made a costly careless mistake (such as marking an answer choice that you didn't mean to mark). This quick double check should more than pay for itself in caught mistakes for the time it costs.

⌀ PACE YOURSELF

It's easy to be overwhelmed when you're looking at a page full of questions; your mind is confused and full of random thoughts, and the clock is ticking down faster than you would like. Calm down and maintain the pace that you have set for yourself. Especially as you get down to the last few minutes of the test, don't let the small numbers on the clock make you panic. As long as you are on track by monitoring your pace, you are guaranteed to have time for each question.

⌀ DON'T RUSH

It is very easy to make errors when you are in a hurry. Maintaining a fast pace in answering questions is pointless if it makes you miss questions that you would have gotten right otherwise. Test writers like to include distracting information and wrong answers that seem right. Taking a little extra time to avoid careless mistakes can make all the difference in your test score. Find a pace that allows you to be confident in the answers that you select.

9

⏱ Keep Moving

Panicking will not help you pass the test, so do your best to stay calm and keep moving. Taking deep breaths and going through the answer elimination steps you practiced can help to break through a stress barrier and keep your pace.

Final Notes

The combination of a solid foundation of content knowledge and the confidence that comes from practicing your plan for applying that knowledge is the key to maximizing your performance on test day. As your foundation of content knowledge is built up and strengthened, you'll find that the strategies included in this chapter become more and more effective in helping you quickly sift through the distractions and traps of the test to isolate the correct answer.

Now that you're preparing to move forward into the test content chapters of this book, be sure to keep your goal in mind. As you read, think about how you will be able to apply this information on the test. If you've already seen sample questions for the test and you have an idea of the question format and style, try to come up with questions of your own that you can answer based on what you're reading. This will give you valuable practice applying your knowledge in the same ways you can expect to on test day.

Good luck and good studying!

Reading

Being able to read well is very important. In fact, without good reading skills it's nearly impossible to do well in other areas of school. In order to be able to properly understand the material in textbooks for subjects such as math, social studies, and science, we must first be able to read the book.

This part of the assessment will measure your reading comprehension, which is just a fancy way of saying your ability to understand what you read. First you'll read a long passage about a village and how they dealt with a monster, and you'll answer 10 questions about it. After that you'll take a practice test of 40 questions, based on several short reading passages. Don't rush through the reading; take your time so you can thoroughly understand what you've read.

In China, New Year's Day is a day for great celebrations. People have big parades, and some of them dress up like a monster called Nian. Almost every family glues red paper to their front doors, keeps the lights on in every room of the house until after midnight, and lights fireworks. This Chinese folk tale explains why they do these things.

How Nian Was Defeated

Chinese New Year Lion Dance
Costume

[1] Once upon a time, near the village of Taohun (Peach Blossom), there lived a huge beast at the bottom of the sea. His name was Nian, and once a year, on New Year's Day, he would come forth out of the sea for one day. After spending all year at the bottom of the ocean, Nian was very hungry. He would eat just about everything he could see. He ate the crops, and he ate the cows, pigs and horses. He ate pets, too. He still wasn't satisfied, though, so he would even eat human beings. Nian especially loved to eat children. If he couldn't find anything to eat, he would get so angry he would destroy everything in his path.

11

2 The people who lived in Taohun were very afraid of Nian. So on New Year's Eve, the day before Nian's arrival, they would flee the village so he wouldn't eat them. The entire village would head to the top of the faraway mountains so that Nian couldn't find them. If they had animals, they would try to take them with them. Every year, though, Nian managed to catch and eat some of the slowest villagers. All year long the villagers lived in dread, knowing that Nian would come out of the ocean on New Year's Day. Even if they managed to avoid being eaten, when they came back to the village they would have to rebuild everything Nian had destroyed.

3 One year an old beggar wandered into the village on New Year's Eve. He went from house to house asking for a bite to eat, but everyone ignored him. They were terrified of the monster, and they were hurrying as fast as they could to get ready to flee the village. Finally an old lady who lived right by the ocean felt sorry for the beggar. She gave him a bite to eat, but then warned him to flee. "Don't you know what day it is tomorrow? Get to the mountains before Nian eats you!"

4 But the old beggar wasn't scared. Instead, he smiled mysteriously. When the woman asked him how he could smile at a time like this, he simply replied, "Ma'am, if you will shelter me in your house for one evening, I will see to it that Nian never terrorizes the village again." The old woman looked at him like he was crazy. Before long it would be dark, and there wasn't much time to spare. "Look, you can't stay in my house. Nian will be coming soon, so you must flee for your life!" But the old man didn't say anything; he just kept smiling mysteriously. Finally the woman decided that there was no more time to argue with him, and she shook her head sadly as she walked out of the house and headed for the mountains. There was nothing more she could do. If the old beggar was foolish enough to stay in her house, he would be sorry.

5 Soon enough, everyone in the village was gone, except for the old beggar in the house. They had all fled to the mountains for safety. At one second past midnight, Nian rose from the bottom of the ocean, just as he did every year. The first house he came to was the old lady's, and he prepared to knock it down in search of something to eat. But just as he started to run toward the door, he noticed something was different this year. There was red paper glued to the door. He was scared of the color red. The house was lit up in every room, and that frightened him even more. Then fireworks started going off, which terrified him. Quivering like a leaf, Nian tucked his tail between his legs and ran back into the ocean.

6 The next day all the people of the village came home. They were shocked to discover that there was no damage to the village at all. They were puzzled and happy at the same time, and they all began to ask each other why Nian hadn't destroyed the village this year. The old lady told them about the strange beggar, and the promise he had made to her. Filled with curiosity and excitement, everyone ran over to the old lady's house. They saw the red paper on the door, all the candles burning in the house, and the used fireworks in the yard. They wondered what it could mean. Then the old beggar came out of the house and explained to them that Nian was afraid of lights, the color red, and loud noises. After that, every year on New Year's Eve, the people of Taohun glued red paper to their doors, lit candles in every room, and set off fireworks to keep Nian away, and he never troubled them again.

SAMPLE QUESTIONS

1. In paragraph 1, which word means the same thing as *sea*?

_____

2. Is this story true?

_____

3. In which country do you think Peach Blossom is located? How did you decide that?

_____

_____

4. Why was the old beggar smiling mysteriously?

_____

_____

5. In paragraph 5, what does *quivering* mean?

_____

6. What does *Taohun* mean in English? How do you know?

_____

_____

7. In paragraph 2, what does *dread* mean?

_____

8. What is the central lesson of this story?

_____

9. Which of these books does this story have the most in common with?

    a. The Story of George Washington
      b. The History of the United States
      c. The Legend of Paul Bunyan
      d. How to Play Baseball

10. Do you think the beggar had any trouble getting the people of Taohun to give him food after what happened? Explain your answer.

_____

_____

ANSWERS

1. *ocean*

2. No; it's a folk tale, and folk tales aren't true. And there are no monsters who come out of the ocean once a year and eat people.

3. China. We can assume it's China because we're told it's a Chinese folk tale, and it's the explanation for the ways people in China celebrate New Year's Day.

4. He was smiling mysteriously because he knew the secret of how to defeat Nian, so he wasn't scared.

5. shaking or trembling

6. *Peach Blossom*. We know this because *Peach Blossom* appears in parentheses right after the word *Taohun*. This is the author's way of telling us what *Taohun* means in English.

7. great fear, terror

8. Even though the story isn't true, it still has a central lesson or point. The central lesson of the story is how the customs of Chinese New Year's celebrations came about.

9. c –This story is a myth and so is *The Legend of Paul Bunyan*, while all the other books contain true stories.

10. Answers can vary, but most likely the old beggar had no trouble getting food in the future because the villagers regarded him as a hero because he had defeated the monster that had terrorized them for years.

Practice Test

Reading

Questions 1-3 pertain to the folktale "The Lion and the Mouse" by Aesop:

A Lion was awakened from sleep by a Mouse running over his face. Rising up angrily, the Lion caught the Mouse and was about to kill him, when the Mouse piteously entreated, saying: "If you would only spare my life, I would be sure to repay your kindness." The Lion laughed and let him go. It happened shortly after this that the Lion was caught by some hunters, who bound him by strong ropes to the ground. The Mouse, recognizing his roar, came and gnawed the rope with his teeth, and set the Lion free, exclaiming:

"You ridiculed the idea of my ever being able to help you, not expecting to receive from me any repayment of your favor; now you know that it is possible for even a Mouse to confer benefits on a Lion."

1. How did the Mouse know that the Lion was in trouble if the Lion let the Mouse go?
   a. Another mouse told him.
   b. Another lion told him.
   c. He heard the Lion's roar.
   d. He heard the steps of the hunters.

2. The Lion learns an important lesson at the end of the story. If a mouse crawls over the Lion's face in the future, what will the Lion do?
   a. The Lion will kill the Mouse.
   b. The Lion will let the Mouse go.
   c. The Lion will be caught by hunters.
   d. The Lion will roar and scare the Mouse away.

3. The Lion lets the Mouse go after laughing about how small the Mouse is. What does this show about the Lion's character?
   a. He is proud, but good at heart.
   b. He pretends to be good, but is really bad.
   c. He likes to laugh a lot.
   d. He likes to let mice go.

Questions 4-6 pertain to the following excerpt from Sarah, Plain and Tall by Patricia MacLachlan:

"Did Mama sing every day?" asked Caleb. "Every-single-day?" He sat close to the fire, his chin in his hand. It was dusk, and the dogs lay beside him on the warm hearthstones.

"Every-single-day," I told him for the second time this week. For the twentieth time this month. The hundredth time this year? And the past few years?

"And did Papa sing, too?"

"Yes. Papa sang, too. Don't get so close, Caleb. You'll heat up."

15

He pushed his chair back. It made a hollow scraping sound on the hearthstones. And the dogs stirred. Lottie, small and black, wagged her tail and lifted her head. Nick slept on.

I turned the bread dough over and over on the marble slab on the kitchen table.

"Well, Papa doesn't sing anymore," said Caleb very softly. A log broke apart and crackled in the fireplace. He looked up at me. "What did I look like when I was born?"

"You didn't have any clothes on," I told him.

"I know that," he said.

"You looked like this." I held the bread dough up in a round pale ball.

"I had hair," said Caleb seriously.

"Not enough to talk about," I said.

"And she named me Caleb," he went on, filling in the old familiar story.

"I would have named you Troublesome," I said, making Caleb smile.

"And Mama handed me to you in the yellow blanket and said..." He waited for me to finish the story. "And said...?"

I sighed. "And Mama said, 'Isn't he beautiful, Anna?'"

"And I was," Caleb finished.

Caleb thought the story was over, and I didn't tell him what I had really thought. He was homely and plain, and he had a terrible holler and a horrid smell. But these were not the worst of him. Mama died the next morning. That was the worst thing about Caleb.

"Isn't he beautiful, Anna?" her last words to me. I had gone to bed thinking how wretched he looked. And I forgot to say good night.

I wiped my hands on my apron and went to the window. Outside, the prairie reached out and touched the places where the sky came down. Though the winter was nearly over, there were patches of snow everywhere. I looked at the long dirt road that crawled across the plains, remembering the morning that Mama had died, cruel and sunny.

They had come for her in a wagon and taken her away to be buried. And then the cousins and aunts and uncles had come and tried to fill up the house. But they couldn't.

Slowly, one by one, they left. And then the days seemed long and dark like winter days, even though it wasn't winter.

And Papa didn't sing.

4. In the excerpt above, this is how Anna describes the prairie: "Outside, the prairie reached out and touched the places where the sky came down." What does this say about the prairie?

   a. The prairie is alive.
   b. The prairie likes to touch the sky.
   c. The sky is falling towards the prairie.
   d. The prairie is a wide, open place.

5. If you could draw Anna's thoughts on a timeline, would they travel in a straight line?

   a. Yes, because Sarah, Plain and Tall takes place in the present.
   b. No, because Anna remembers her mother's death in between her chores.
   c. Yes, because Anna's mother is dying while she is doing the chores.
   d. No, because Anna is only thinking about the future.

6. Who is the "I" who is telling the story?

   a. Anna
   b. Caleb
   c. Sarah
   d. The reader

7. What is the difference between a story like *The Lion and the Mouse* and a story like *Sarah, Plain and Tall?*

   a. *The Lion and the Mouse* is a serious story, and *Sarah, Plain and Tall* is a funny story.
   b. *Sarah, Plain and Tall* teaches a moral lesson, and *The Lion and the Mouse* does not.
   c. *Sarah, Plain and Tall* could take place in real life; *The Lion and the Mouse* could not.
   d. *The Lion and the Mouse* and *Sarah, Plain and Tall* are the same kind of story.

Questions 8-13 pertain to the following excerpt from So You Want to Be President? By Judith St. George:

Every single President has taken this oath: "I do solemnly swear (or affirm) that I will faithfully execute the office of President of the United States, and will to the best of my ability, preserve, protect, and defend the Constitution of the United States."

Only thirty-five words! But it's a big order if you're President of this country.

Abraham Lincoln was tops at filling that order. "I know very well that many others might in this matter or as in others, do better than I can," he said. "But... I am here. I must do the best I can, and bear the responsibility of taking the course which I feel I ought to take."

That's the bottom line. Tall, short, fat, thin, talkative, quiet, vain, humble, lawyer, teacher, or soldier—this is what most of our Presidents have tried to do, each in his own way. Some succeeded. Some failed. If you want to be President—a good President—pattern yourself after the best. Our best have asked more of themselves than they thought they could give. They have had the courage, spirit, and will to do what they knew was right. Most of all, their first priority has always been the people and the country they served.

8. When the narrator is talking about "You," who is the narrator speaking to?
   a. The President of the United States
   b. Someone who wants to be President of the United States.
   c. You and only you
   d. Anyone who reads the book.

9. If you were to draw a picture of all of the presidents of the United States, what would they look like?
   a. They would all look the same.
   b. They would all look very different.
   c. Their faces would be on a dollar bill.
   d. They would look like Abraham Lincoln.

10. "Only thirty-five words! But it's a big order if you're President of this country." Here, the word "but" contrasts something in the first sentence and something in the second. What is the author contrasting?
   a. The difference between a good president and a bad president.
   b. The difference between a large number of words and a small order.
   c. The difference between a small number of words and a big order.
   d. There is no contrast between the first and second sentence.

11. According to the excerpt, the best presidents have had one thing in common: "Most of all, their first priority has always been the people and the country they served." What does the word *priority* mean here?
   a. Whatever is most important to the presidents.
   b. Whatever is least important to the presidents.
   c. Whatever the presidents like doing the most.
   d. Whatever the presidents like doing the least.

12. For whom is this book written?
   a. Only people who are trying to be president.
   b. Only people who are able to become president.
   c. Anyone who wants to know what being president means.
   d. Anyone who has been President of the United States.

13. According to the Presidential Oath, what is the most important thing that the President has to defend?
   a. The land that the United States owns
   b. The whole world and everyone in it
   c. The people in the United States government
   d. The Constitution of the United States

14. Marty and Freya practice sign language frequently: they meet every Monday, Tuesday, Wednesday, Thursday, and Friday to practice. What does the word *frequently* mean?
   a. Never
   b. Always
   c. Often
   d. Sometimes

15. The following sentence contains a wrong word: "Talia stopped skipping in the street when she saw a horse and chart racing toward her." Which word would best replace the incorrect word in the sentence?

 a.   Cart
 b.   Chase
 c.   Chat
 d.   Chart

16. You and a classmate are reading the fairy tale *Rumpelstiltskin*. You think the most important part of the story is the beginning. Your classmate says that the most important part of the story is the ending. What is the best argument to support your opinion?

 a.   The beginning is longer than the ending.
 b.   The beginning is where we meet our main characters.
 c.   The ending is boring and the beginning is exciting.
 d.   Your classmate doesn't know the story as well as you do.

17. You write the following sentence: "In the summer, I pick corn and beans and peas and not squash." What is the best way to use linking words to improve this sentence?

 a.   In the summer, I pick corn, beans, peas, and not squash.
 b.   In the summer, I pick corn, beans, peas, and squash.
 c.   In the summer, I pick corn and beans, peas and not squash.
 d.   In the summer, I pick corn, beans, and peas, but not squash.

18. You are adapting a fairy tale called *The Snow Queen*. What is the most important thing to remember when you describe the character of the Snow Queen to your readers?

 a.   Describe how she looks
 b.   Describe where she lives
 c.   Describe what she wears
 d.   Describe how she acts

19. When Barry's parents told him that he was going to have a baby brother, he forgot to put his shoes on when he left for school! What do you think Barry was feeling?

 a.   Barry felt so surprised that he forgot to put his shoes on.
 b.   Barry felt so confident that he didn't need shoes.
 c.   Barry hated putting shoes on, whether he was going to have a brother or not.
 d.   Barry felt feverish, so he didn't put any shoes on.

20. Identify the misspelled word in the following sentence: "Mara was friendly, but because she studied ancient Egypt, her neighbors thought she was wierd."

 a.   Friendly
 b.   Ancient
 c.   Neighbors
 d.   Wierd

21. You are working on an essay on alligators and want to write your final paragraph. What information should you include?

 a. What alligators are
 b. Where alligators are born
 c. Why alligators are not crocodiles
 d. Why alligators are important

22. You are keeping a journal in class of interesting things that happen each day. One day, you are sitting in class and you can't think of anything to write. What should you do?

 a. Write about something exciting that happened yesterday.
 b. Skip the journal entry for that day.
 c. Read about what happened in the world today, and write about that.
 d. Make up something interesting that happened to you.

23. An adjective is a part of speech that describes a noun. Identify the adjective(s) in the following sentence: "Michael sees a tiny rip in his father's favorite hat."

 a. Tiny
 b. Favorite
 c. Both A and B
 d. Hat

24. The old nursery rhyme goes, "Hickory dickory dock / The mouse ran up the clock." What would the rhyme say if the mouse had a family who ran up the clock with him?

 a. Hickory dickory dock / The mouses ran up the clock.
 b. Hickory dickory dock / The mice ran up the clock.
 c. Hickory dickory dock / The mices ran up the clock.
 d. Hickory dickory dock / The mouse ran up the clock.

25. Your teacher has just finished discussing the past, present, and future tenses with your class. However, you still have trouble telling the tenses apart. What is the best question to ask your teacher?

 a. "Can you give us an example from a book that we're reading?"
 b. "What is the past tense?"
 c. "Can you repeat that?"
 d. "Why can't I understand this lesson?"

26. You think that Charlotte from *Charlotte's Web* is a hero. Your classmate thinks that a creature as small as a spider cannot be a hero. What is the best way to explain why Charlotte is a hero?

 a. Give examples of small heroes from other books you have read.
 b. Tell your classmate that no one else in the book is a hero, so Charlotte has to be.
 c. Give examples of Charlotte's heroism throughout the book.
 d. Tell your classmate that he or she is not always right in class discussions.

27. Charles Dickens wrote, "A loving heart is the truest wisdom." What kind of a noun is _wisdom_?

a. A person
b. A place
c. A thing
d. An idea

28. Maurice wants to be a violinist when he grows up. How will he tell this to his parents?

a. "When I grow up, I will play the violin."
b. "When I grow up, I play the violin."
c. "When I grow up, I played the violin."
d. "When I grow up, I have played the violin."

29. During summer vacation, you and your parents visit Mexico. When you go back to school, you want to tell everyone what Mexico was like. Which answer lists the details of your trip in order, from the most important to the least important?

a. I wore summer clothes, I drank a beverage called horchata, I climbed the Pyramid of the Sun, and I talked to a Mexican boy about what life is like in the desert.
b. I climbed the Pyramid of the Sun, I drank a beverage called horchata, I wore summer clothes, and I talked to a Mexican boy about what life is like in the desert.
c. I wore summer clothes, I climbed the Pyramid of the Sun, I drank a beverage called horchata, and I talked to a Mexican boy about what life is like in the desert.
d. I talked to a Mexican boy about what life is like in the desert, I climbed the Pyramid of the Sun, I drank a beverage called horchata, and I wore summer clothes.

Questions 30 and 31 pertain to the poem "At the Sea-Side" by Robert Louis Stevenson:

When I was down beside the sea

A wooden spade they gave to me

To dig the sandy shore.

My holes were empty like a cup.

In every hole the sea came up,

Till it could come no more.

30. If you were reading this poem out loud, how many times would you pause your reading between one line and another?

a. None
b. Three
c. Two
d. One

31. Choose the two lines from the poem that form a complete sentence.

a. When I was down beside the sea/ A wooden spade they gave to me
b. To dig the sandy shore. / My holes were empty like a cup.
c. My holes were empty like a cup. / In every hole the sea came up,
d. In every hole the sea came up, / Till it could come no more.

32. Choose the correct pair of adjectives to replace the underlined words in the following sentence: "I saw the <u>funny</u> clowns at the fair on Tuesday; it was the <u>fun</u> time I have ever had."

a. funniest / most fun
b. funnier / funner
c. funniest / funnest
d. most funny / most fun

33. You decide to write a letter to the president. You want to make sure that the address on the envelope is written correctly. Which is the best way to write the address for the White House?

a. The White House
1600 Pennsylvania Avenue NW
Washington DC 20500
b. The White House,
1600 Pennsylvania Avenue NW,
Washington DC 20500
c. The White House
1600 Pennsylvania Avenue NW
Washington, DC 20500
d. The White House
1600 Pennsylvania Avenue NW
Washington DC 20500

34. When you have a spoken argument with someone and you get angry, you raise your voice. What is the correct way to show this in writing?

a. Put one exclamation point at the end of your sentence.
b. Put several exclamation points at the end of your sentence.
c. Put every single word in capital letters.
d. Put every single word in bold.

35. An *academy* is a place where students go for advanced education. Mr. Rowland is an *academic*. What is Mr. Rowland's job?

a. Teacher
b. Policeman
c. Computer repairman
d. Secretary

36. Carla says to Manuel, "The mail might be late tomorrow." Manuel says to Joseph, "The mail will be late tomorrow." Who is more certain that the mail will be late?

a. Carla
b. Manuel
c. Joseph
d. None of the above

37. A family is having dinner at a rectangular table. Mom and Dad are sitting on one side of the table, and Grandpa and Grandma are sitting on the other side. Mom and Dad are sitting...
   a. Across from Grandpa and Grandma.
   b. Behind Grandpa and Grandma.
   c. Beside Grandpa and Grandma.
   d. Next to Grandpa and Grandma.

38. Rewrite the following sentence without a comma: "Because it rained heavily in the summer, flowers sprang up almost overnight."
   a. Flowers sprang up almost overnight although it rained heavily in the summer.
   b. Because it rained heavily in the summer flowers sprang up almost overnight.
   c. Flowers sprang up almost overnight because it rained heavily in the summer.
   d. Flowers sprang up almost overnight if it rained heavily in the summer.

Please use the image below to answer Question 39:

39. Imagine that this illustration is on the front cover of a book. Which of the following is the most likely title of the book?
   a. The Polar Express
   b. A Child's Garden of Verses
   c. The Wind in the Willows
   d. The Tale of Peter Rabbit

40. Choose the correct verb form of "to carry" to complete the following sentence: "A week ago, when the old fisherman walked home, he [to carry] with him the largest trout in town."
   a. A week ago, when the old fisherman walked home, he carries with him the largest trout in town.
   b. A week ago, when the old fisherman walked home, he carry with him the largest trout in town.
   c. A week ago, when the old fisherman walked home, he carryed with him the largest trout in town.
   d. A week ago, when the old fisherman walked home, he carried with him the largest trout in town.

Written Expression

How well can you express yourself in writing? In other words, are you good at clearly getting a message across to others by using good writing? You'll need to be good at expressing yourself in writing if you want to do well in school. This ability is also very important in other areas of life, too. This exercise will help you improve your Written Expression skills.

1. My neighbor mumbles a lot, so I sometimes _____ her.
   a. ununderstand
   b. disunderstand
   c. misunderstand
   d. reunderstand

2. Her _____ under stress helped everyone else relax.
   a. calmitude
   b. calmless
   c. calmness
   b. calmy

3. Put a slash (/) between syllables in the word below.

quarterback

4. _____ are words that tell us more about a person, place or thing.
   a. Nouns
   b. Verbs
   c. Adjectives
   d. Adverbs

5. The plural form of *calf* is _____.

6. Underline the abstract noun in the sentence below:

Micah, your duty will be to sweep the floor.

7. Is the underlined word in the sentence below a concrete noun or an abstract noun? In the blank space, write A for abstract or C for concrete:

Having good <u>health</u> is better than having a lot of money.

_____

8. Fill in the blank space of the second sentence using the correct tense of the verb underlined in the first sentence:

<u>Buy</u> me a hot dog while you're at the concession stand.

Yesterday I _____ a new comic book with my allowance.

9. There are three main verb tenses: past, present, and future. Fill in the blank below with the verb tense that is missing:

will think   think   _____

10. Mrs. Jones and Ms. Sanchez both _____ 3rd grade at Eastside Elementary.

(teach)(teaches)

11. The team won _____ last three games.

(its)(they)(theirs)(us)

For questions 12 and 13:

An adjective is listed before each sentence. In each sentence, fill in the blank with the correct form of the adjective, either comparative or superlative. (Answers can be one or two words.)

12. ATHLETIC

I like sports a little, but my brother is _____ than I am.

13. SAD

That was the _____ story I've ever read

For questions 14 and 15:

In front of each sentence is an adverb. Fill in the blank in each sentence using the correct form of the adverb. Answers can be one or two words.

14. WELL

We played well, but unfortunately the other team played _____ .

15. PROMPTLY

Class, this assignment needs to be completed _____ than last week's.

For questions 16 and 17:

Read each sentence and decide if the sentence is a compound sentence, or a complex sentence. Write your answer in the blank space below the sentence.

16. Brian is going to the museum and Wendy is going to the bookstore.

_____

17. Although he really didn't want to, Kent agreed to wear a tie to the restaurant.

_____

For questions 18 and 19:

Each pair of sentences expresses two thoughts, followed by a coordinating conjunction. Rewrite them using one compound sentence, using the coordinating conjunction shown.

18. You can eat lunch now. You can eat lunch later. OR

_____

19. You should study hard. You can pass your test. SO

_____

For questions 20 and 21:

> Each pair of sentences expresses two thoughts, followed by a subordinating conjunction. Rewrite them using one complex sentence, using the subordinating conjunction shown.

20. You must clean your room. You may go outside and play. BEFORE

_____

21. Watch out for traffic. You ride your bike.   WHILE

_____

For questions 22 and 23:

> The sentence sounds awkward the way it is written. Rewrite it using a possessive.

22. Let's say hello to the mom of Tanequa.

_____

23. This is the uniform that belongs to Jack.

_____

For questions 24 and 25

> Unscramble the mixed up word and write it in the blank below.

24. A talking fish? That's mispsiboel!

_____

25. I'll have to ask my parents, but I bporyalb will be able to attend your birthday party.

_____

For questions 26 and 27:

> Add a suffix to the base word listed in front of the sentence to make a new word to complete the sentence.

26. INTEREST

I'm sorry, but I just didn't find the book to be very _____ .

27. REPLACE

Class, Ms. Brown is sick today, so I will be her _____ .

26

28. Which of these sentences is the most appropriate?

    a. In the middle of a daydream, Becky was startled by the classroom bell.
    b. In the middle of a daydream, Becky was shocked by the classroom bell.
    c. In the middle of a daydream, Becky was terrified by the classroom bell.

29. Which sentence best expresses the idea that a comedian was extremely funny?

    a. The comedian was humorous.
    b. The comedian was hilarious.
    c. The comedian was amusing.

30. Which sentence is the best for describing the story of Paul Bunyan and Babe?

    a. It is a tall tale
    b. It is a lie.
    c. It is a falsehood.

31. Which of these sentences sounds nicest?

    a. Oh, what an obese little baby!
    b. Oh, what an overweight little baby!
    c. Oh, what a chubby little baby!

For questions 32 and 33:

Each sentence has one underlined word, which contains a prefix or a suffix. Use your knowledge of the root word to figure out the definition of the new word, and choose the correct answer.

32. Charles Lindbergh made the first solo <u>transatlantic</u> flight.

    a. across the Atlantic Ocean
    b. into the Atlantic Ocean
    c. under the Atlantic Ocean

33. My little brother gets <u>hyperactive</u> when he eats too much sugar.

    a. not active
    b. less active
    c. very active

For questions 34 and 35:

Using a suffix, fill in the blank with letters to change the word to match the definition shown.

34. state of being aware = aware_____

35. possessing caution = cauti_____

Mathematics

All four digit whole numbers have a thousands, hundreds,

tens and a ones place.

Thousands	Hundreds	Tens	Ones
1	1	2	4

= 1,124

Count the groups, then write the numbers.

1. = 1,347

2. = _____

3. = _____

4. = _____

5. = _____

To add multiple digit numbers together, start in the ones place and then use basic addition rules. When the number equals ten or more the first digit carries over to the next spot. This is called **regrouping**.

	Hundreds	Tens	Ones
Step 1: Add the digits in the ones column.		8	5
	+	1	7
			2

	Hundreds	Tens	Ones
Step 2: Carry the 1 over to the top of the tens column.		1	
		8	5
	x	1	7
		①	2

	Hundreds	Tens	Ones
Step 3: Add all the digits in the tens column together.		1	
		8	5
	x	1	7
	1	0	2

Solve the two-digit addition problems below.

1. $\begin{array}{r} 65 \\ +14 \\ \hline 79 \end{array}$

2. $\begin{array}{r} 35 \\ +54 \\ \hline \end{array}$

3. $\begin{array}{r} 11 \\ +51 \\ \hline \end{array}$

4. $\begin{array}{r} 42 \\ +35 \\ \hline \end{array}$

5. $\begin{array}{r} 89 \\ +10 \\ \hline \end{array}$

6. $\begin{array}{r} 25 \\ +81 \\ \hline \end{array}$

7. $\begin{array}{r} 47 \\ +31 \\ \hline \end{array}$

8. $\begin{array}{r} 12 \\ +26 \\ \hline \end{array}$

9. $\begin{array}{r} 25 \\ +44 \\ \hline \end{array}$

10. $\begin{array}{r} 51 \\ +27 \\ \hline \end{array}$

11. $\begin{array}{r} 19 \\ +10 \\ \hline \end{array}$

12. $\begin{array}{r} 13 \\ +34 \\ \hline \end{array}$

To subtract and borrow, start with the ones column. If the bottom number is of a greater value, you have to borrow from the next column.

Step 1: If the bottom number is a greater value than the top number, you need to borrow.	Tens | Ones	**Step 2:** Borrow 10 from the next column. Reducing the 8 to 7 and increasing 4 to 14. Now we are ready to subtract.	Tens | Ones	**Step 3:** Finish by subtracting the numbers in the tens column.	Tens | Ones
	8 | 4 − 1 | 9		7 8 | ¹4 − 1 | 9 | 5		7 8 | ¹4 − 1 | 9 6 | 5

Solve the two-digit subtraction problems below.

1. 23
   − 10
   ‾‾‾‾
    13

2. 86
   − 81

3. 24
   − 19

4. 65
   − 29

5. 58
   − 21

6. 42
   − 12

7. 38
   − 16

8. 37
   − 15

9. 61
   − 34

10. 57
   − 43

11. 85
   − 26

12. 82
   − 39

The answer to a multiplication problem is called the **product**.

Switching the order doesn't matter. The product will always be the same.

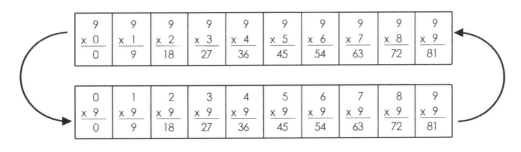

Find the product.

1. 9 x 1 — 9	**2.** 4 x 9	**3.** 8 x 7	**4.** 9 x 9	**5.** 3 x 7	**6.** 5 x 8	**7.** 9 x 1
8. 3 x 1	**9.** 6 x 4	**10.** 2 x 1	**11.** 6 x 9	**12.** 2 x 8	**13.** 7 x 5	**14.** 9 x 5
15. 9 x 4	**16.** 4 x 9	**17.** 0 x 9	**18.** 6 x 3	**19.** 3 x 7	**20.** 2 x 5	**21.** 3 x 9

Divide each problem.

1. $10\overline{)100}$ with quotient 10

2. $6\overline{)24}$

3. $5\overline{)25}$

4. $9\overline{)45}$

5. $6\overline{)42}$

6. $25\overline{)25}$

7. $25\overline{)125}$

8. $11\overline{)110}$

9. $7\overline{)21}$

10. $6\overline{)36}$

A fraction names a part of a whole. It can also be used to name a part of a group or set.

Fractions are made up of two parts: the **numerator** and the **denominator**.

○ ○ ⟶ $\frac{1}{4}$ ← The numerator is the number of shaded objects.
○ ○   ← The denominator is the total number of objects.

Write what fraction of each set is shaded in.

1. ○ ○
  ○ ●   = $\frac{1}{4}$

2. ● ○ ○
  ○ ○ ○   = ☐

3. ● ● ○ ○
  ○ ○ ○ ○   = ☐

4. ○○○○○
  ○○○○○
  ○●●●●   = ☐

5. = ☐

6. = ☐

7. = ☐

8. = ☐

Use the graph to answer the questions.

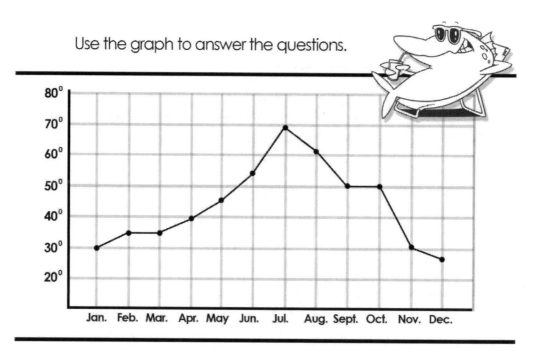

1. What was the coldest month? __December__

2. What was the hottest month? _____

3. What was the temperature in March? _____

4. About how many degrees was the difference between the coldest and hottest months? _____

5. What was the temperature in November? _____

6. Did it become hotter or colder from April to May? _____

7. Did the temperature change from September to October? _____

8. Which month was colder, January or December? _____

Each coin has its own value.

= 1 penny = 1¢

= 1 nickel = 5¢

= 1 dime = 10¢

= 1 quarter = 25¢

We add the coins together to get the values.

Each bill has its own value.

 = One Dollar

= $1

 = Five Dollars

= $5

 = Ten Dollars

= $10

 = Twenty Dollars

= $20

We add the bills together to get the values.

Write the correct amount of money for each question.

1.  $ 1.41

2.  $_____

3.  $_____

4.  $_____

5.  $_____

6.  $_____

Perimeter is the distance around an object.
Find the perimeter of each object by adding all the sides.
Write out the equation.

1.

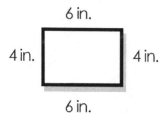

6 in.

4 in.   4 in.

6 in.

4 + 6 + 4 + 6 = 20 in.

2.

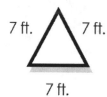

7 ft.   7 ft.

7 ft.

3.

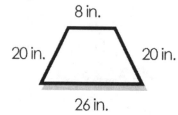

8 in.

20 in.   20 in.

26 in.

4.

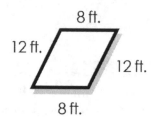

8 ft.

12 ft.   12 ft.

8 ft.

5.

6 in.   6 in.

9 in.   9 in.

6 in.

6.

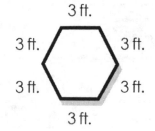

3 ft.

3 ft.   3 ft.

3 ft.   3 ft.

3 ft.

1 foot = **12** inches
1 yard = **3** feet or **36** inches
1 mile = **1,760** yards

Answer the questions and tell whether each question should
use measurement units of a foot, yard or mile

---

1. The length of a soccer field should be measured in __yards__ .

2. Tommys' height should be measured in _____.

3. The distance from home to school is measured in _____.

4. The basketball goal is 10 _____ tall.

5. Steven can jump 3 _____.

6. The distance between the earth and moon is measured
   in _____.

7. The tree in the yard is 22 _____ tall

8. A football field is measured in _____.

9. Roads are measured in _____.

10. A 12 inch ruler is a _____ long.

ANSWERS

Place Values and Number Sense

1. 1,347

2. 3,232

3. 2,459

4. 4,157

5. 3,175

Addition

1. 79

2. 89

3. 62

4. 77

5. 99

6. 106

7. 78

8. 38

9. 69

10. 78

11. 29

12. 47

Subtraction

1. 13

2. 5

3. 5

4. 36

5. 37

6. 30

7. 22

8. 22

9. 27

10. 14

11. 59

12. 43

Multiplication

1. 9

2. 36

3. 56

4. 81

5. 21

6. 40

7. 9

8. 3

9. 24

10. 2

11. 54

12. 16

13. 35

14. 45

15. 36

16. 36

17. 0

18. 18

19. 21

20. 10

21. 27

Division

1. 10

2. 4

3. 5

4. 5

5. 7

6. 1

7. 5

8. 10

9. 3

10. 6

Fractions

1. 1/4

2. 2/6

3. 2/8

4. 4/15

5. 6/8

6. 7/10

7. 5/12

8. 9/15

Graphing

1. December

2. July

3. About 35 degrees

4. 40-45 degrees

5. 30 degrees

6. hotter

7. no

8. December

Counting Money

1. $1.41

2. $3.12

3. $7.61

4. $30.18

5. $25.87

6. $35.33

Geometry | Measurements

1. 4 + 6 + 4 +6 = 20 in

2. 7 + 7 + 7 = 21ft

3. 8 + 20 + 20 + 26 = 74in

4. 12 + 8 + 12 + 8 = 40ft

5. 6 + 6 + 9 +6 + 9 = 36in

6. 3 + 3 + 3 + 3 + 3 + 3 = 18ft

1. yards

2. feet

3. miles

4. feet

5. feet

6. miles

7. feet

8. yards

9. miles

10. foot

1. Interpret 6 × 4 in a real world context.
   a. A family with 4 children has a total of 6 people in it.
   b. There are 6 cookies, and you eat 4 of them.
   c. You buy 6 binders for $4 each.
   d. You have $6, and your mom gives you $4 more.

2. Interpret 24 ÷ 8 in a real world context.
   a. A total of 24 slices of pizza are divided among 8 hungry people.
   b. There are 24 houses, and each has 8 windows.
   c. You have 24 baseball cards, and you buy 8 more.
   d. Your vacation lasts 8 days, and each day has 24 hours.

3. Ms. Nelson evenly distributes 32 crayons to 8 kindergarteners. How many crayons does each student get?
   a. 3 crayons
   b. 4 crayons
   c. 6 crayons
   d. 8 crayons

4. Calculate the missing number in 4 × □ = 20.
   a. 4
   b. 5
   c. 6
   d. 7

5. Which equation means the same as 9 × 15 = 135?
   a. $3 \times 6 \times 15 = 135$
   b. $9 + (3 + 5) = 135$
   c. $9 \times 5 \times 10 = 135$
   d. $15 \times 9 = 135$

6. Calculate 24 ÷ 6.
   a. 2
   b. 3
   c. 4
   d. 6

7. Calculate 8 × 9.
   a. 63
   b. 64
   c. 69
   d. 72

8. Leslie spends $4 on ice cream. She only has $7 left. How much did she have before she bought the ice cream?
   a. $3
   b. $4
   c. $10
   d. $11

9. You spent $21 to buy 7 raffle tickets. How much did each raffle ticket cost?

a. $2
b. $3
c. $4
d. $5

10. Examine the multiplication table. If two numbers are multiplied together, when will the result be odd?

a. When both numbers are even
b. When both numbers are odd
c. When neither number is odd
d. When one number is even and one number is odd

11. Round 437 to the nearest ten.

a. 400
b. 430
c. 440
d. 500

12. Calculate 381 + 54.

a. 335
b. 435
c. 721
d. 921

13. Calculate 4 × 60.

a. 18
b. 24
c. 180
d. 240

14. Which fraction is represented by the darkly shaded area below?

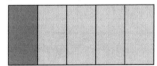

a. $\frac{1}{5}$
b. $\frac{4}{5}$
c. $\frac{5}{4}$
d. $\frac{5}{1}$

45

15. Which point represents the fraction $\frac{1}{4}$ on the number line below?

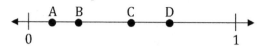

   a. Point A
   b. Point B
   c. Point C
   d. Point D

16. Which point represents the fraction $\frac{3}{5}$ on the number line below?

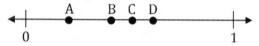

   a. Point A
   b. Point B
   c. Point C
   d. Point D

17. Which fraction is equivalent to the one represented by the darkly shaded area below?

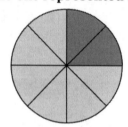

   a. $\frac{1}{8}$
   b. $\frac{1}{4}$
   c. $\frac{1}{3}$
   d. $\frac{3}{4}$

18. Which fraction is equivalent to $\frac{4}{6}$?

   a. $\frac{1}{3}$
   b. $\frac{1}{2}$
   c. $\frac{2}{3}$
   d. $\frac{2}{1}$

19. Which fraction is equivalent to 5?

   a. $\frac{1}{5}$
   b. $\frac{1}{1}$
   c. $\frac{5}{5}$
   d. $\frac{5}{1}$

46

20. Compare the fractions $\frac{3}{5}$ and $\frac{2}{5}$.

    a. $\frac{3}{5} > \frac{2}{5}$

    b. $\frac{3}{5} = \frac{2}{5}$

    c. $\frac{3}{5} < \frac{2}{5}$

    d. None of the above

21. Compare the fractions $\frac{2}{5}$ and $\frac{2}{7}$.

    a. $\frac{2}{5} > \frac{2}{7}$

    b. $\frac{2}{5} = \frac{2}{7}$

    c. $\frac{2}{5} < \frac{2}{7}$

    d. None of the above

22. Karen takes a 30-minute lunch break starting at 12:15. At what time should she come back from her lunch break?

    a. 12:30

    b. 12:35

    c. 12:40

    d. 12:45

23. A penny has a mass of about 3 grams. What is the approximate mass of 6 pennies?

    a. 9 grams

    b. 12 grams

    c. 15 grams

    d. 18 grams

24. A wooden board has a mass of 12 kg. If you cut off 4 kg, what is the mass of the remaining piece?

    a. 3 kg

    b. 6 kg

    c. 8 kg

    d. 9 kg

25. Which bar graph best represents the data set below?

Average Yearly Rainfall	
City	Rainfall
Chicago	36 in.
Honolulu	18 in.
New York, NY	50 in.
Phoenix	8 in.
Washington, DC	39 in.

a.

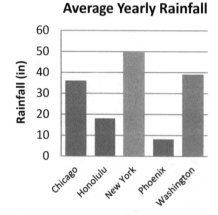

b.

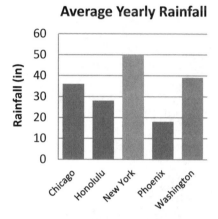

c.

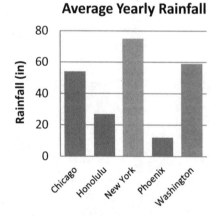

d.

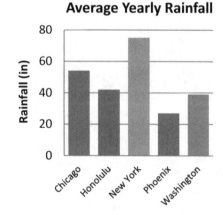

26. Which line plot best represents the data set below?

Lengths of Common Objects	
Object	**Length**
AAA Battery	4.1 cm
Glue	7.9 cm
Paperclip	4.8 cm
Tape	10 cm

a.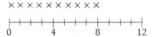

b.

c.

d.

27. The sides of a square are 1 cm long. What is the area of the square?

    a. 1 cm
    b. 1 m
    c. $1\ cm^2$
    d. $1\ m^2$

28. A rectangular figure is covered by 25 unit squares. What is the area of the figure?

    a. 5 units
    b. 25 units
    c. 5 square units
    d. 25 square units

29. The figure below is divided into unit squares. What is the area of the figure?

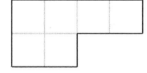

    a. 1 square unit
    b. 3 square units
    c. 5 square units
    d. 6 square units

30. Calculate the area of the rectangle below.

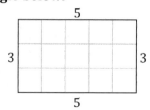

  a. 8 square unit
  b. 10 square units
  c. 15 square units
  d. 16 square units

31. Calculate the area of the rectangle below.

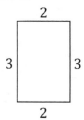

  a. 5 square units
  b. 6 square units
  c. 8 square units
  d. 10 square units

32. The dimensions of a rectangular check are 3 in. by 6 in. What is its area?
  a. 9 in2
  b. 12 in2
  c. 15 in2
  d. 18 in2

33. What equation does the figure below represent?

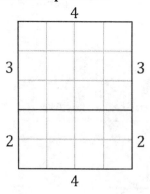

  a. $4 \times (3 + 2) = (4 \times 3) + (4 \times 2)$
  b. $4 \times 5 = (2 \times 3) + (2 \times 4)$
  c. $5 \times (3 + 2) = (4 \times 3) + (4 \times 2)$
  d. $5 \times 4 = (5 \times 2) + (5 \times 2)$

34. Calculate the area of the figure below.

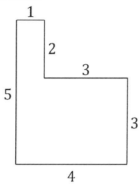

   a.   12 square units
   b.   14 square units
   c.   16 square units
   d.   20 square units

35. Calculate the area of the figure below.

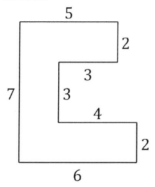

   a.   28 square units
   b.   32 square units
   c.   36 square units
   d.   40 square units

36. A rectangle is 7 units long and has a perimeter of 22 units. What is its width?

   a.   4 units
   b.   8 units
   c.   12 units
   d.   15 units

37. Three shapes are shown below. What do they all have in common?

Equilateral
Triangle

Square

Regular
Pentagon

a. They all have right angles
b. They all have sides of equal length.
c. They all have three sides.
d. All of the above

38. The square below is divided into 9 parts with equal areas. What fraction of the total area of the square does the shaded area take up?

a. $\frac{1}{9}$

b. $\frac{1}{6}$

c. $\frac{1}{3}$

d. $\frac{2}{3}$

Science

Learning about science is both fun and educational. The world is made up of all kinds of interesting plants and animals, in all shapes and sizes. We learn about these in science, and we also learn about things like stars and planets, weather, oceans, gravity, atoms, and much more. For many students, science is their favorite subject to study at school. Here are some questions about science that can help you improve your skills in this area.

Directions: Use the information below and your knowledge of science to answer questions 1 – 3.

An explorer finds two islands in the Pacific Ocean with very different terrains and climates. One island is wet and full of plants and fruit, whereas the other is dry and barren except for a few plants that grow edible seeds with very hard shells. Nevertheless, she finds birds on the two islands that have many similar traits.

1. Which of the following is the best explanation for the similarity in the birds' traits?
   a. The birds on the two islands are closely related.
   b. The birds attained similar traits through parallel evolution.
   c. Something that the birds are eating gives them these similar traits.
   d. The similar traits must be a coincidence; there is no reason birds on different islands should be similar.

2. Over time, the birds on the two islands may become more different. Which of the following is most likely to happen to the birds on the dry island?
   a. They will grow larger bills to help them crack the hard seeds.
   b. They will lose their wings and become unable to fly.
   c. They will grow webbed feet to swim in the ocean.
   d. They will grow larger and become carnivorous.

3. Which of the following words describes the process of organisms having traits passed down from their parents?
   a. Adaptation
   b. Diversity
   c. Inheritance
   d. Variation

4. Two magnets exert forces on a third magnet that is originally at rest. What information about the forces is necessary to know whether or not the third magnet will start moving?
   a. How big the forces are
   b. What direction the forces are acting in
   c. Both A and B
   d. No further information is necessary; if there are two forces acting on an object, it will always move.

5. Which of the following does the force between two magnets *not* depend on?
   a. The strength of the magnets
   b. The orientation of the magnets
   c. The distance between the magnets
   d. The altitude of the magnets above the Earth's surface

6. If a force acts on a moving object, what effect will it have?

a. The object will slow down.
b. The object will speed up.
c. The object will change direction.
d. Any of the above are possible.

7. During what season of the year are days the longest and nights the shortest?

a. Spring
b. Summer
c. Fall
d. Winter

8. A group of students around the US decides to measure the length of the day (the time between sunrise and sunset) in different cities to see if the days are longer in some cities than others. For the data to be most useful, which of the following should the students be sure to do?

a. Take measurements on the same day of the year.
b. Take measurements on different days of the year.
c. Use different clocks to measure the time of sunrise and sunset.
d. Ignore any data that don't match what they expect to find.

Directions: *Use the information below and your knowledge of science to answer questions 9 – 10.*

Two streams run through a field. One stream is badly polluted, and the other is cleaner. An ecologist measures the average weight of frogs in the two rivers and finds the following information:

	Average weight in grams
Polluted stream	18
Clean stream	25

9. Which of the following statements is best supported by the data?

a. The pollution has no effect on the ecosystem.
b. The pollution has stunted the growth of the frogs in the polluted stream.
c. The pollution has killed off most of the frogs in the polluted stream.
d. The pollution is actually healthy for the frogs.

10. What is the best way for the ecologist to have measured the average weight of the frogs in each stream?

a. The ecologist measured the weight of one random frog and assumed it was equal to the average.
b. The ecologist picked a frog that looked about average and measured its weight.
c. The ecologist added together the weights of many frogs and divided by the number of frogs.
d. The ecologist measured the weights of three frogs, and took the one in the middle.

11. Which of the following is a *reversible* physical change?

    a. Burning paper
    b. Cooking meat
    c. Melting ice
    d. Shattering a rock

12. What property of an object is measured in degrees Celsius?

    a. Length
    b. Weight
    c. Hardness
    d. Temperature

Directions: Use the information below and your knowledge of science to answer questions 13 – 15.

A meteorologist measures the amount of rain in her city in different months of the year, and she compiles the following data:

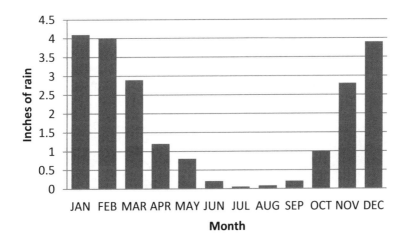

13. According to the meteorologist's data, about how many inches of rain fell in the month of March?

    a. 1.0
    b. 2.9
    c. 5.8
    d. 11.0

14. In which month did the least rain fall?

    a. January
    b. April
    c. July
    d. October

15. What term describes the patterns in the weather in different areas and its changes over time?

 a. Climate
 b. Ecology
 c. Precipitation
 d. Prediction

Directions: *Use the information below and your knowledge of science to answer questions 16 – 19.*

A student decides to try putting different chemicals on plants to see if any of them help the plant grow. He treats various specimens of the same type of plant with different chemicals and obtains the following data:

CHEMICAL:	HEIGHT (in inches):
None	30
Chemical #1	26
Chemical #2	25
Chemical #3	36
Chemical #4	12

16. According to the student's data, which chemical helped the plant to grow the best?

 a. Chemical #1
 b. Chemical #2
 c. Chemical #3
 d. Chemical #4

17. What could the student do differently to be more certain that this chemical actually helped the plant's growth?

 a. Do more tests with different chemicals.
 b. Do multiple trials with the same chemicals.
 c. Measure the plants again after more time has passed.
 d. Find out what the chemical is made of.

18. In order to properly compare the plant's growth, the student also measured one plant to which he did not add any extra chemicals. Which of the following terms describes this plant?

 a. Control
 b. Dependent variable
 c. Independent variable
 d. Proportion

19. Which of the following statements is best supported by the student's data?

 a. Plants need water and light to grow.
 b. Organisms are able to cause changes in their environments.
 c. Organisms' traits can give them advantages for survival and reproduction.
 d. The traits that an organism develops can be affected by its environment.

20. Sound is an example of which of the following?

    a. A force
    b. A liquid
    c. A solid
    d. A wave

21. A loud sound is played next to a thin metal rod. Which of the following is most likely to happen?

    a. The rod will expand.
    b. The rod will vibrate.
    c. The rod will bend toward the sound.
    d. The rod will bend away from the sound.

Directions: Use the information below and your knowledge of science to answer questions 22 – 24.

The town of Harborton is subject to frequent thunderstorms, with lots of heavy rain. Flooding and lightning strikes are frequent problems in the town.

22. Which of the following places would be the safest place to build a house in Harborton?

    a. On the banks of a river
    b. In a canyon
    c. On a sandy hillside
    d. On a rocky hilltop

23. Many buildings in Harborton are fitted with lightning rods. How do lightning rods protect against lightning strikes?

    a. The lightning hits the rod and is trapped inside it.
    b. The lightning hits the rod and is conducted safely into the ground.
    c. The lightning is repelled by the rod and will not strike the house.
    d. The lightning is reflected by the rod back into the sky.

24. If you're in Harborton when a lightning storm is approaching, where is the safest place for you to be?

    a. In an enclosed building
    b. In an open field
    c. Swimming in a lake
    d. Under a tree

25. A species that no longer exists is said to be

    a. Evolved
    b. Extinct
    c. Prehistoric
    d. Symbiotic

26. One piece of evidence that lets us know more about species from the past and their environments is the remains of organisms that have been turned to stone by geologic processes. These remains are known as

    a. Faults
    b. Fossils
    c. Geodes
    d. Vestigial

27. Probably the most famous animals that are no longer around are dinosaurs. Actually, some descendants of the dinosaurs are still around today (birds), but the rest of the dinosaurs died out. Not counting birds, about how long ago did dinosaurs live?

    a. Hundreds of years
    b. Thousands of years
    c. Millions of years
    d. Billions of years

Directions: *Use the information below and your knowledge of science to answer questions 28 – 30.*

> An explorer on a distant planet finds an alien machine. One large part of the machine is a large ball on a rod that revolves quickly around the machine. The explorer decides to time how long it takes the ball to make one complete revolution. He starts a stopwatch when the ball is directly in front of him, and he finds that the ball is in front of him again when the stopwatch shows 12 minutes, again at 24 minutes, and again at 36 minutes.

28. What would he expect the stopwatch to show when the ball is in front of him again?

    a. 48 minutes
    b. 1 hour and 12 minutes (72 minutes)
    c. 2 hours
    d. 12 hours

29. Based on the ball's movement, is there a force acting on it?

    a. No; the ball's motion is constant, so there is no force acting on it.
    b. Yes; the ball is moving, so there must be a force acting on it.
    c. Yes; the ball's direction of motion is changing, so there must be a force acting on it.
    d. More measurements are necessary to determine whether or not there is a force acting on the ball.

30. In case the ball's motion changes with temperature, the explorer decides to measure the temperature. What instrument would he use for this?

    a. Barometer
    b. Centimeter
    c. Kilometer
    d. Thermometer

Social Studies

Social studies classes cover many different topics. They include learning where people live, how they get along with each other, and how they organize their governments. Along with these subjects, students also learn about history, law, money, and religion, and how they have helped make different people groups what they are today. These social studies questions cover these topics and more, and will help you get more out of your classes.

1. Which of the following continents is entirely in the Southern Hemisphere?

   a. Europe
   b. South America
   c. Australia
   d. Africa

2. Which landform is surrounded by water on three sides?

   a. Peninsula
   b. Isthmus
   c. Cliff
   d. Island

3. Before the American Revolution, the states were known by another name. What was that name?

   a. Territories
   b. Colonies
   c. Regions
   d. Villages

4. Which branch of government is responsible for making laws?

   a. Executive
   b. Judicial
   c. Legislative
   d. Federal

5. Which document announced that the American people no longer considered themselves part of Great Britain?

   a. Bill of Rights
   b. Constitution
   c. Gettysburg Address
   d. Declaration of Independence

6. Which type of landform would only be found in far northern climates?

   a. Tundra
   b. Valley
   c. Steppe
   d. Canyon

7. In what city did the colonists dump tea in order to oppose new taxes from Great Britain?

    a. New York
    b. Yorktown
    c. Concord
    d. Boston

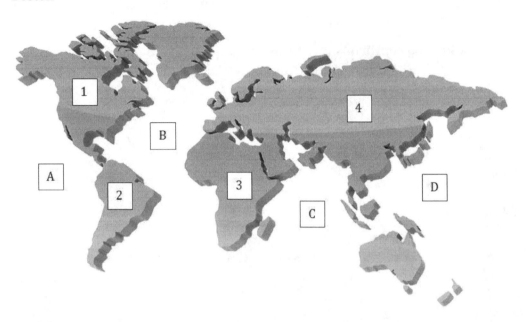

Directions: Use the map above and your knowledge of social studies to answer questions 8 through 10.

8. Which continent is identified by the number 3 above?

    a. South America
    b. Europe
    c. Asia
    d. Africa

9. Which of the following continents is NOT identified by a number above?

    a. North America
    b. Australia
    c. Africa
    d. Asia

10. Which ocean is represented by two different letters above?

    a. Atlantic
    b. Arctic
    c. Indian
    d. Pacific

11. How many senators does each state send to Congress?

    a. 2
    b. 3
    c. 4
    d. 5

12. How long is a single term that a senator in Congress serves?

    a. 4 years
    b. 6 years
    c. 7 years
    d. 8 years

13. How is the number of representatives that each state has in the House of Representatives decided?

    a. Coin toss
    b. Number of counties
    c. Population of state
    d. Size of capital city

14. Which of the following is NOT a natural resource?

    a. Forest
    b. City
    c. River
    d. Coal

15. An entrepreneur is defined as someone who does which of the following?

    a. Runs for public office
    b. Purchases stock in the stock market
    c. Runs a restaurant
    d. Starts a business

16. When George Washington was president of the United States, who served as vice president?

    a. John Adams
    b. Thomas Jefferson
    c. James Madison
    d. Abraham Lincoln

17. Which branch of government determines whether or not laws follow the requirements of the US Constitution?

    a. Executive
    b. Judicial
    c. Legislative
    d. Federal 18

18. Which of the following is another word for *money*?

    a. Circulation
    b. Currency
    c. Exchange
    d. Tax

19. Which of the following would be considered a need?

    a. Candy bar
    b. Dishwasher
    c. New car
    d. Fresh water

20. Which of the following is an example of bartering?

    a. Richard offers to mow his neighbor's lawn for free.
    b. Jillian saves up her allowance money to buy a video game.
    c. Mickey sets up a lemonade stand and charges $.15 per cup.
    d. Kristina cleans the ballet studio in exchange for classes.

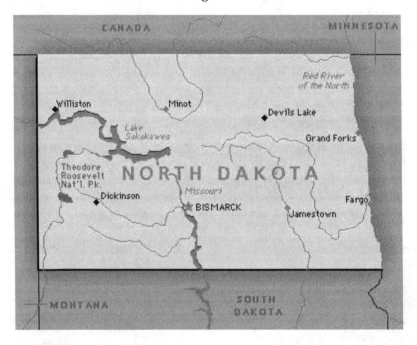

Directions: Use the map above and your knowledge of social studies to answer questions 21 through 23.

21. To travel from the city of Williston to the city of Minot, which direction would you go?

    a. North
    b. South
    c. East
    d. West

22. From the city of Minot, you travel directly south to the first city shown on the map. Then, you travel directly west. In which city do you end up?

    a. Bismarck
    b. Dickinson
    c. Jamestown
    d. Grand Forks

23. Which of the following is NOT shown on the map above?

a. Lake
b. Mountain
c. National park
d. River

24. Which branch of government has the power of veto?

a. Executive
b. Judicial
c. Legislative
d. Federal

25. Which of the following is an example of importing?

a. A country experiencing a drought brings in food from countries around it.
b. A doctor visits another country to treat patients who cannot get medical care.
c. A business owner begins selling products to customers in other states.
d. A car manufacturer purchases new parts from a factory in a nearby town.

26. Which of the following is an example of exporting?

a. An artist donates a new painting to raise money for an auction.
b. A country with an abundance of silver sells it to other countries.
c. A celebrity orders a specially made gown from a designer.
d. A boy gives away his lunch in exchange for his friend's lunch.

27. Which of the following is an example of a producer?

a. Sallie purchases all her fresh fruits and vegetables at the farmer's market.
b. Donald checks out the books at his local library for all his reading wants.
c. Caroline only shops at local shops to support businesses in her community.
d. Marla runs a bakery and focuses on making cakes for weddings.

28. Which of the following men was president during the Civil War?

a. Thomas Jefferson
b. Ulysses S. Grant
c. Abraham Lincoln
d. Andrew Johnson

29. Which of the following is an example of a human resource?

a. Computer program
b. House painter
c. Ballpoint pen
d. Silver dollar

30. Which of the following was NOT one of the 13 original states?

a. New Hampshire
b. Massachusetts
c. Florida
d. New York

Vocabulary

There's a name for all the words you are familiar with and know how to use – it's called your vocabulary. The more words you know, the larger your vocabulary is. You may not realize it, but you already know thousands of words, and you use hundreds of them every day when you talk to your friends, classmates and family members.

It's important to have a large vocabulary, because if you have trouble recognizing words and knowing how to use them it will be very difficult to learn new information in any area. Also, knowing a lot of words can help you figure out the meanings of new words when you come across them without having to stop and look up the definition. The following exercise is designed to measure how big your vocabulary is.

For each sentence, choose the answer that is the closest in meaning to the word in italics.

1. Is there any *advantage* in this for you?
    a. something harmful
    b. something helpful
    c. something hard
    d. something easy

2. You have all the *ability* you need.
    a. money
    b. movement
    c. skill
    d. wish

3. That book is *ancient*.
    a. brand new
    b. hard to read
    c. expensive
    d. very old

4. His *triumph* didn't last long.
    a. victory
    b. temper tantrum
    c. loss
    d. talent

5. My uncle is *feeble*.
    a. old
    b. strong
    c. lazy
    d. weak

6. His statement made me *pause*.
    a. stop for a short time
    b. work harder than ever
    c. become very angry
    d. dig fast

7. That building is _vacant_.

- a. big
- b. brick
- c. empty
- d. new

8. I'm starting to get _drowsy_.

- a. angry
- b. bored
- c. hungry
- d. sleepy

9. On the phone, he sounded _distant_.

- a. rich
- b. far away
- c. very close
- d. very loud

10. My neighbor is _odd_.

- a. normal
- b. strange
- c. short
- d. tall

11. After he sits too long, Grandpa looks very _rigid_.

- a. wrinkled
- b. rough
- c. stiff
- d. old

12. It looks _shallow_ from here.

- a. deep
- b. not deep
- c. skinny
- d. very heavy

13. _Grasp_ the stick, Billy.

- a. drop
- b. reach
- c. hold
- d. throw

14. It will _decay_ soon.

- a. fall apart
- b. pick up
- c. rebuild
- d. move to another place

15. Did you *consider* your mother?

    a. think about

    b. sit down next to

    c. speak to

    d. ignore

16. Her movements were *swift*.

    a. fast

    b. slow

    c. crooked

    d. straight

17. What is the *moisture* level?

    a. dryness

    b. redness

    c. wetness

    d. darkness

18. You must *observe* carefully.

    a. write

    b. count

    c. fight

    d. watch

19. That is a *rare* breed of dog.

    a. handsome

    b. weak

    c. hard to find

    d. strange

20. They will *perhaps* come to visit this month.

    a. for sure

    b. twice

    c. never

    d. maybe

21. He said he's not *certain*.

    a. hungry

    b. sure

    c. sick

    d. upset

22. You will *regret* this.

    a. feel sadness about

    b. feel happiness about

    c. not remember

    d. do over

23. My friend is _furious_.

- a. very funny
- b. very sad
- c. very angry
- d. very hungry

24. _Reply_ as soon as possible.

- a. come over
- b. give an answer
- c. try again
- d. cancel a meeting

25. The game will _occur_ this Saturday.

- a. take place
- b. be on TV
- c. be enjoyable
- d. cost a lot of money

26. I took a walk along the _ocean_.

- a. pond
- b. lake
- c. river
- d. sea

27. That dog is _enormous_.

- a. tiny
- b. huge
- c. speedy
- d. unfriendly

28. That gemstone is quite _brilliant_.

- a. expensive
- b. cheap
- c. bright
- d. dark

29. Did you _purchase_ that?

- a. borrow
- b. steal
- c. loan
- d. buy

Spelling

Spelling is a very important skill to have. It can seem hard at first. If you work at it, though, it can become easy. That's because there are some rules you can use to help you. Not all words follow the spelling rules, but most of them do. The most important thing is to practice, practice, practice. If you keep at it, you can become a very good speller.

Spelling Exercise

Each question contains four words. If one of them is misspelled, circle it. If they are all spelled correctly, circle NO MISTAKES.

1.	gras	light	spray	strike	NO MISTAKES
2.	fish	follo	stairs	when	NO MISTAKES
3.	deap	organ	smash	tutor	NO MISTAKES
4.	boy	fastened	herry	pale	NO MISTAKES
5.	throne	student	stubborn	deel	NO MISTAKES
6.	they	berst	dream	agree	NO MISTAKES
7.	meal	smell	toogether	choose	NO MISTAKES
8.	sumthing	told	watched	suddenly	NO MISTAKES
9.	face	aunt	dirty	questun	NO MISTAKES
10.	belong	nickel	boddle	different	NO MISTAKES
11.	explore	finul	fever	phone	NO MISTAKES
12.	else	wheather	central	natural	NO MISTAKES
13.	restle	thought	telescope	claws	NO MISTAKES
14.	whale	tinsul	embrace	benefit	NO MISTAKES
15.	storage	recite	stomach	arange	NO MISTAKES
16.	bargain	midst	collection	obzerve	NO MISTAKES
17.	piramid	chocolate	wonderful	geometry	NO MISTAKES
18.	comfortable	sixth	referee	falt	NO MISTAKES
19.	machete	sheeth	reptile	contagious	NO MISTAKES
20.	suport	cajole	orange	position	NO MISTAKES
21.	celebration	Wensday	exciting	witnessed	NO MISTAKES
22.	colonel	continuity	independence	mischievious	NO MISTAKES
23.	glisten	approximate	thourully	carelessly	NO MISTAKES
24.	wondrous	appearance	fernish	doggedly	NO MISTAKES

Capitalization

Capitalization is an important part of written English. By using capital letters properly we can show respect for others. We can make some things stand out as important, or let the reader know when we're discussing the title of something such as a play or a book. We can also make it clear that a new sentence has started, and much more. Besides, if we never capitalized anything, and used only lower case letters all the time, reading would soon become boring.

There are rules to follow when it comes to what words should be capitalized so there's no need for guessing when it comes to capitalization. These 20 questions will measure how well you know the rules of capitalization.

Read each numbered item, and then decide if it's capitalized correctly, or incorrectly. If it's capitalized incorrectly, choose the answer which contains the mistake. If it's capitalized correctly, choose NO MISTAKES. Sentences may contain words that aren't capitalized that should be, or words that are capitalized that shouldn't be, or both.

1. (title) Five Things You Should Know About Rattlesnakes

   a. Five things
   b. You Should Know
   c. About Rattlesnakes
   d. NO MISTAKES

2. **That's easy for you to say, mom!**

   a. That's easy
   b. for you
   c. to say, mom!
   d. NO MISTAKES

3. **Cheaper by the dozen is a very funny movie.**

   a. Cheaper by the dozen
   b. is a
   c. very funny movie.
   d. NO MISTAKES

4. **In October of 1871, fire destroyed much of Chicago, illinois.**

   a. In October of 1871,
   b. fire destroyed much
   c. of Chicago, illinois.
   d. NO MISTAKES

5. **Is doctor Jones available to see me now?**

   a. Is doctor Jones
   b. available to
   c. see me now?
   d. NO MISTAKES

69

6. **"be careful, Frank!" yelled Coach Johnson.**

    a. "be careful,
    b. Frank!" yelled
    c. coach Johnson.
    d. NO MISTAKES

7. **After the game, a Reporter interviewed the coach.**

    a. After the game,
    b. a Reporter interviewed
    c. the coach.
    d. NO MISTAKES

8. **Last year on vacation, we went to yellowstone national Park.**

    a. Last year on vacation,
    b. we went to
    c. yellowstone national Park.
    d. NO MISTAKES

9. **Dr. Bramley is chairman of the Department of Astronomy.**

    a. Dr. Bramley is
    b. chairman of the
    c. Department of Astronomy.
    d. NO MISTAKES

10. **Muslims believe in allah and follow the teachings of the Koran.**

    a. Muslims believe in allah
    b. and follow the teachings
    c. of the Koran.
    d. NO MISTAKES

11. **Bill Gates is the founder of the company called microsoft.**

    a. Bill Gates is the
    b. founder of the
    c. company called microsoft.
    d. NO MISTAKES

12. **During world war II, my grandfather lived in France.**

    a. Back during world war II,
    b. my grandfather lived
    c. in France.
    d. NO MISTAKES

13. **Christmas and new year's day are always one week apart.**

    a. Christmas and
    b. new year's day are
    c. always one week apart.
    d. NO MISTAKES

14. (letter salutation) Dear reverend Swanson,

    a. Dear
    b. reverend
    c. Swanson
    d. NO MISTAKES

15. In my opinion, no salad is complete without italian dressing.

    a. In my opinion,
    b. no salad is complete
    c. without italian dressing.
    d. NO MISTAKES

16. (title) Here's Why you Should Exercise Every Day

    a. Here's Why
    b. you Should Exercise
    c. Every Day
    d. NO MISTAKES

17. My sister was born during a Blizzard on January 27th.

    a. My sister was born
    b. during a Blizzard
    c. on January 27th.
    d. NO MISTAKES

18. My dad reads the *New York times* every day.

    a. My dad reads the
    b. *New York times*
    c. every day.
    d. NO MISTAKES

19. (title) The Hound Of The Baskervilles

    a. The Hound
    b. Of The
    c. Baskervilles
    d. NO MISTAKES

20. I didn't realize I was speeding, officer Smith.

    a. I didn't realize
    b. I was speeding,
    c. officer Smith.
    d. NO MISTAKES

Punctuation

Punctuation is very important in written English. When sentences aren't punctuated correctly, readers get confused and messages get mixed up. You want to make sure you get your point across when you write something. To do that, you must use good punctuation. This exercise will test your punctuation skills.

The sentence in each question may contain a punctuation error. If there is an error, select the answer choice which contains the error. If there is no error, select NO MISTAKES.

1. Boise Idaho is the biggest city I've ever visited.

    a. Boise Idaho is
    b. the biggest city
    c. I've ever visited.
    d. NO MISTAKES

2. "Mom doesn't want us to have snacks before supper, Billy reminded Joanie.

    a. "Mom doesn't want us
    b. to have snacks before supper,
    c. Billy reminded Joanie.
    d. NO MISTAKES

3. Freida asked, "What time does the bus usually get here"

    a. Freida asked, "What
    b. time does the bus
    c. usually get here"
    d. NO MISTAKES

4. Sir, Pedro exclaimed, "you dropped your wallet."

    a. Sir, Pedro exclaimed,
    b. "you dropped
    c. your wallet."
    d. NO MISTAKES

5. The capital of France is Paris which has over 10 million residents.

    a. The capital of France
    b. is Paris which has over
    c. 10 million residents.
    d. NO MISTAKES

6. "Are those your sunglasses?" Molly asked?

    a. "Are those
    b. your sunglasses?"
    c. Molly asked?
    d. NO MISTAKES

7. "James and Kirk," said Mr. Brown "you need to see me after class."

    a. "James and Kirk,"

    b. said Mr. Brown "you need

    c. to see me after class."

    d. NO MISTAKES

8. Des, Moines is the biggest city in Iowa.

    a. Des, Moines is

    b. the biggest city

    c. in Iowa.

    d. NO MISTAKES

9. Dad said, "Lets go to the beach this Saturday."

    a. Dad said, "Lets go

    b. to the beach

    c. this Saturday."

    d. NO MISTAKES

10. "I don't think that's a very good idea Mabel," her mother replied.

    a. "I don't think that's

    b. a very good idea Mabel,"

    c. her mother replied.

    d. NO MISTAKES

11. Does anyone know what time it is.

    a. Does anyone

    b. know what

    c. time it is.

    d. NO MISTAKES

12. Ms. Ramirez said "Class, it's time for a pop quiz."

    a. Ms. Ramirez said

    b. "Class, it's time for

    c. a pop quiz."

    d. NO MISTAKES

13. The bus should be here in just a few minutes?

    a. The bus should

    b. be here in just

    c. a few minutes?

    d. NO MISTAKES

14. "Mom," Janice asked, "when are Grandma and Grandpa going to get here."

    a. "Mom," Janice asked,

    b. "when are Grandma and

    c. Grandpa going to get here."

    d. NO MISTAKES

15. "I wouldn't do that if I were you", Dad said to Mike.

    a. "I wouldn't do that

    b. if I were you",

    c. Dad said to Mike.

    d. NO MISTAKES

16. The days of the week are, Sunday, Monday, Tuesday, Wednesday, Thursday, Friday, and Saturday.

    a. The days of the week are,

    b. Sunday, Monday, Tuesday, Wednesday,

    c. Thursday, Friday, and Saturday.

    d. NO MISTAKES

17. If you don't succeed the first time try again.

    a. If you don't

    b. succeed the first

    c. time try again.

    d. NO MISTAKES

18. "Stop this instant." the policeman exclaimed.

    a. "Stop this instant."

    b. the policeman

    c. exclaimed.

    d. NO MISTAKES

19. Mom said to Deepak "What did you say?"

    a. Mom said

    b. to Deepak

    c. "What did you say?"

    d. NO MISTAKES

20. I'm going you're going, Heather's going, and Eliza's going.

    a. I'm going you're going,

    b. Heather's going,

    c. and Eliza's going.

    d. NO MISTAKES

Practice Test Answers and Explanations

Reading

1. C: The Mouse hears the Lion's roar and comes to the rescue.

2. B: The Lion learns that even a small Mouse can be helpful. Since learning this lesson, the Lion will let other mice go in the future.

3. A: Although the Lion is too proud for his own good, his letting the Mouse go shows that he is good at heart.

4. D: Anna is using figurative language to describe how the prairie is a wide, open space. Although the prairie is described as if it were a person, it is just Anna's imagination.

5. B: Anna's thoughts are jumping all over the place, from the chores she is doing at the moment to her mother's death and back again.

6. A: Anna is telling the story in the first person. We know she is the one telling the story because she remembers her mother saying, "Isn't he beautiful, Anna?" when talking about her brother, Caleb.

7. C: *Sarah, Plain and Tall* is a work of historical fiction, which means it could have taken place in the real world long ago. *The Lion and the Mouse* is a folktale in which animals talk; it is not meant to be realistic.

8. D: The narrator is talking to anyone who is reading the book.

9. B: The narrator tells us that presidents have been "Tall, short, fat, thin, talkative, quiet, vain, humble, lawyer, teacher, or soldier." Even though they all have held the same office, they are very different people.

10. C: The word *only* in the sentence means that the number of words is small, and yet the job of President is a big responsibility.

11. A: A *priority* is something that comes first because it matters more to you than anything else. The best presidents' priorities have always been the people and the country they served.

12. C: Anyone who wants to know about what it means to be president should read this book.

13. D: The most important job that the President has is to uphold the Constitution. The Constitution is what makes the United States the country that it is.

14. C: Marty and Freya don't meet every day, but they meet most days to practice, so this means that they meet often, or *frequently.*

15. A: A horse and cart were racing toward Talia, not a horse and chart.

16. B: This answer is a good explanation, because it is based on a fact, and it makes logical sense. The other answer choices are either opinions, or they don't make any sense.

75

17. D: You only need one *and* at the end of a list, but when you add an action that does not fit the list (not picking squash), you need to use a different linking word, *but*.

18. D: *Character* refers to how a person behaves or acts, particularly in different places or around different people. The other answer choices are things you might talk about, but they don't show the Snow Queen's character.

19. A: Barry was so surprised at the news about a baby brother that it made him forget about putting his shoes on.

20. D: *Wierd* should be spelled *weird*.

21. D: Your final paragraph should remind your readers of the overall idea behind your essay. Specific facts and definitions belong in earlier paragraphs.

22. C: Sometimes, interesting things are happening in the world around you that you don't know about until you read about them.

23. C: *Tiny* describes the rip, and *favorite* describes the hat.

24. B: *Mice* is the correct plural form of *mouse*.

25. A: If you don't understand a concept the first time around, it is helpful to learn from an example found in a book that you already know.

26. C: It may be helpful to point out that there have been other small heroes in different books, but you want to explain why Charlotte is a hero. Because you are talking about Charlotte, the best way to explain your point of view to your classmate is to talk about her and the brave things she does.

27. D: Wisdom is not something that you can see or touch, but rather an idea that you can think about.

28. A: *Will play* is the simple future tense for the verb *to play*.

29. D: The most important details of a travel trip come from talking to the people who live there.

30. C: There are three full stops, or periods, in the poem. When reading a poem out loud, always pause between sentences. So you would pause twice between the lines. The period at the end wouldn't signal a pause; you would stop completely.

31. D: This answer is a complete thought with a period at the end.

32. A: *Funniest* is the correct way to say *most funny*. On the other hand, *funnest* is not a word; *most fun* is the correct phrase.

33. C: Always put a comma between the city and state, or between the city and the District of Columbia (DC).

34. A: To show anger in writing, the right way is to put one exclamation point at the end of a sentence. Be careful not to overuse exclamation points; if you do, your writing may become hard to read.

35. A: *Academic* and *academy* both have to do with education, which is the job of a teacher.

36. B: *Will* is a stronger word than *might,* because *might* means that the speaker is not sure about what will happen.

37. A: Because Mom and Dad are sitting on the opposite side of the table, they are sitting *across from* Grandma and Grandpa.

38. C: The conjunction *because* moves between the two ideas in the sentence, connecting them together in the place of a comma.

39. B: The image of a child with roses would not go well with a winter story like *The Polar Express,* and there are no willows or rabbits in the illustration. The image on the cover of a book shows what the book is mainly about.

40. D: The past tense of the verb *to carry* is *carried*.

Written Expression

1. C: misunderstand

2. C: calmness

3. quar/ter/back

4. C: Adjectives

5. calves

6. duty

7. A: abstract

8. bought

9. thought

10. teach

11. its

12. more athletic

13. saddest

14. better

15. more promptly

16. compound

17. complex

18. You can eat lunch now, or you can eat lunch later.

19. You should study hard so you can pass your test.

20. Either of these is correct: You must clean your room before you may go outside and play. | Before you may go outside and play, you must clean your room.

21. Either of these is correct: Watch out for traffic while you ride your bike. | While you ride your bike, watch out for traffic.

22. Let's say hello to Tanequa's mom.

23. This is Jack's uniform.

24. impossible

25. probably

26. interesting

27. replacement

28. A: In the middle of a daydream, Becky was startled by the classroom bell.

29. B: The comedian was hilarious.

30. A. It is a tall tale

31. C. Oh, what a chubby little baby!

32. A: across the Atlantic Ocean

33. C: very active

34. awareness

35. cautious

Mathematics

1. C: You can think of 6 × 4 as six groups of four objects. If you buy 6 binders for $4 each, then the total amount of money you spend is $4 + $4 + $4 + $4 + $4 + $4, which is six groups of $4.

2. A: You can think of 24 ÷ 8 as equally dividing 24 objects into eight groups. If 24 slices of pizza are divided between 8 people, then you have to divide the slices into eight groups.

3. B: There are 32 crayons that are evenly divided among 8 students. Therefore, you can find number of crayons each student gets by dividing 32 by 8. The result is 4 crayons each.

4. B: The opposite of multiplication is division. Use division of the product (20) by the known factor (4) to obtain the missing number.

Therefore, 20 ÷ 4 = 5

5. D: The commutative property of multiplication states that the order of the numbers being multiplied does not matter. For instance, 2 × 3 and 3 × 2 are both equal to 6. In the problem, we are given the equation 9 × 15 = 135. Therefore, by the commutative property, 15 × 9 is also equal to 135.

6. C: Division and multiplication are inverse operations, just as subtraction and addition are. To calculate 7 − 3, ask yourself "What number can be added to 3 to get 7?" Since the answer is 4, we know that 7 − 3 = 4.

Similarly, to calculate 24 ÷ 6, ask yourself "What number can be multiplied by 6 to get 24?" By trial-and-error, you can find that 4 × 6 = 24. Therefore, we know that 24 ÷ 6 = 4.

7. D: In the multiplication table, the 8s are 8, 16, 24, 32, 40, 48, 56, 64, 72, 80. Therefore, 8 × 9 = 72.

8. D: To start, let the letter a stand for the amount of money Leslie had before she bought the ice cream (which is what we are looking for). Now we can say that after she spends $4 on ice cream, Leslie has a total of $a − 4$ dollars left. We are also told that she has $7 left after buying ice cream. Therefore, the correct equation is $a − 4 = 7$.

Because addition and subtraction are related, we can calculate a by adding 7 + 4. The answer is 11, which we can check by making sure that 11 − 4 = 7. It works, so Leslie had $11 before she bought the ice cream.

9. B: To start, let the letter b stand for price of each raffle ticket (which is what we are looking for). Now we can say that if you buy 7 raffle tickets, then the total price is $b × 7$. We are also told that you spend a total of $21. Therefore, the correct equation is $b × 7 = 21$.

Because multiplication and division are related, we can calculate b by dividing 21 ÷ 7. The answer is 3, which we can check by making sure that 3 × 7 = 21. It works, so each raffle ticket cost $3.

10. B: Carefully examine the multiplication table and identify some of the products that are odd. For example:

$$3 \times 3 = 9$$

$$3 \times 5 = 15$$

$$5 \times 1 = 5$$

$$7 \times 9 = 63$$

Notice that in all of these cases the numbers being multiplied together are both odd.

11. C: To round to the nearest ten, first look at the digit in the tens place, which is a 3. Thus, if you round 437 *down*, the 3 will stay the same, and the answer will be 430. Conversely, if you round it *up*, the 3 will go up to a 4, and the answer will be 440. Finally, look at the number after the 3, which is a 7. Since it is greater than 5, you should round up. Therefore, the answer is 440.

12. B: Set up the addition vertically, making sure to line up the digits by place value.

```
  381
+  54
  435
```

13. D: Notice that 60 is a multiple of 10; in other words, it has a zero in the ones place. There is a trick to multiplying numbers like this. To multiply 4×60, first multiply 4×6 and then add a zero to the end. Therefore, the answer is 240.

14. A: A fraction $\frac{1}{b}$ can be represented as a whole partitioned (or divided) into b equal parts. For example, if a figure is divided into 2 equal parts, then each part represents $\frac{1}{2}$ of the whole. Notice that the rectangle in the problem is divided into 5 equal parts and one of those parts is shaded. Therefore, it represents the fraction $\frac{1}{5}$.

15. B: If you partition (or divide) the space between 0 and 1 on a number line into b equal parts, then each part has size $\frac{1}{b}$, and the first division to the right of zero represents the point $\frac{1}{b}$. For example, if you divide the space between 0 and 1 on a number line into three equal parts, then each part has size $\frac{1}{3}$ and the first endpoint represents the point $\frac{1}{3}$.

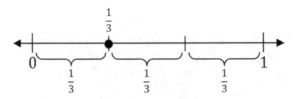

Therefore, to find $\frac{1}{4}$, divide the space between 0 and 1 on a number line into four equal parts. The first endpoint represents $\frac{1}{4}$.

16. D: If you partition (or divide) the space between 0 and 1 on a number line into b equal parts, then the ath division to the right of zero is the point $\frac{a}{b}$. For example, if you divide the space between 0 and 1 on a number line into three equal parts, then the second endpoint represents the point $\frac{2}{3}$.

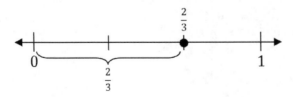

Therefore, to find $\frac{3}{5}$, divide the space between 0 and 1 on a number line into five equal parts. The third endpoint represents $\frac{3}{5}$.

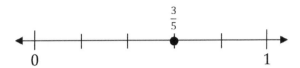

17. B: A fraction can be represented as a whole partitioned (or divided) into equal parts. In addition, two fractions are equivalent if they are the same size. Notice that the circle in the problem is divided into 8 equal parts and two of those parts are shaded. Therefore, the shaded region represents $\frac{2}{8}$. This is equivalent to the fraction $\frac{1}{4}$ as shown by the darkly shaded area in the circles below.

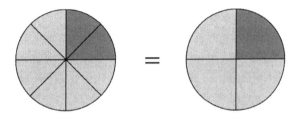

18. C: A fraction can be represented as a whole partitioned (or divided) into equal parts. In addition, two fractions are equivalent if they are the same size. The darkly shaded area below represents the fraction $\frac{4}{6}$.

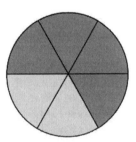

This is equivalent to the fraction $\frac{2}{3}$ as shown by the darkly shaded area below.

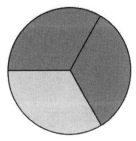

19. D: A whole number a can be expressed as a fraction $\frac{a}{1}$. This is because $\frac{a}{1}$ represents a "divided" into one part. Therefore, 5 is equivalent to the fraction $\frac{5}{1}$.

20. A: A fraction $\frac{a}{b}$ can be represented as a parts of a whole that is partitioned (or divided) into b equal parts. Therefore, if you divide a whole into 5 parts, then 3 of those parts are larger than 2 of them. Thus, the correct answer is $\frac{3}{5} > \frac{2}{5}$ as shown by the figures below.

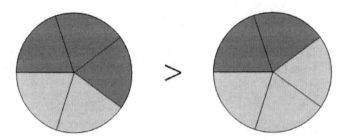

21. A: A fraction $\frac{a}{b}$ can be represented as a parts of a whole that is partitioned (or divided) into b equal parts. Therefore, if you divide a whole into 5 parts, then each part will be larger than if you had divided the whole into 7 parts. Thus, the correct answer is $\frac{2}{5} > \frac{2}{7}$ as shown by the figures below.

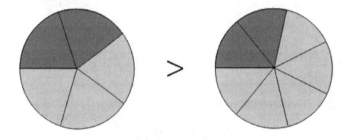

22. D: To calculate when her lunch break finishes, add 30 minutes to the time it starts, 12:15. Since we know that 15 + 30 = 45, the correct answer is 12:45.

23. D: Since each penny has a mass of about 3 grams, you can find the total mass of 6 pennies by adding 3 + 3 + 3 + 3 + 3 + 3. In other words, you have to multiply 3 × 6. Thus, the total mass is 18 grams.

24. C: To find mass of the leftover piece, subtract the mass you cut off from the mass of the original board: 12 − 4. Thus, the mass of the leftover piece is 8 kg.

25. A: To draw a bar graph, first make a title and two axes. For this problem, the vertical axis will have average yearly rainfall (in inches), and the horizontal axis will have the five given cities.

Moreover, notice that the data ranges from 8 in. of rainfall to 50 in. Therefore, for the vertical axis, we can go from 0 to 60 by counting by tens. Set up the bar graph.

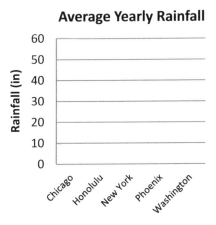

Finally, add a bar for each of the five cities. Using your eye, try to make sure that the bar for Chicago goes up to about 36. Then make a bar for Honolulu that goes up to about 18, and so on.

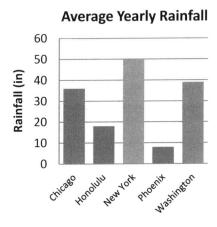

26. B: To draw a line plot, first make a title and two axes. For this problem, the vertical axis will have the four objects, and the horizontal axis will have the length of the objects (in cm). Moreover, notice that the data ranges from 4.1 cm to 10 cm. Therefore, for the vertical axis, we can go from 0 to about 12. Set up the line plot.

Lengths of Common Objects

Battery

Glue

Paperclip

Tape

```
 0        4        8       12
          Length (cm)
```

Finally, add ×'s in horizontal lines for each of the four objects. Put one × for each centimeter. For parts of a centimeter (like the ".1" in 4.1), use a portion of an ×.

Lengths of Common Objects

Battery   × × × × ×

Glue   × × × × × × × ×

Paperclip   × × × × ×

Tape   × × × × × × × × × ×

```
├──┼──┼──┼──┼──┼──┼──┼──┼──┼──┼──┤
0        4        8       12
        Length (cm)
```

27. C: A square with sides of length 1 unit (called a "unit square") has an area of 1 square unit. Since the sides of the unit square in the problem are 1 cm long, its area is 1 square centimeter, notated as 1 cm^2.

28. D: A figure that is covered with n unit squares has an area of n square units. Since the given figure is covered with 25 unit squares, its area is 25 square units.

29. D: A figure that is covered with n unit squares has an area of n square units. Since the given figure is divided into 6 unit squares, its area is 6 square units.

30. C: Notice that the rectangle has already been divided into unit squares. A figure that is divided into n unit squares has an area of n square units. Therefore, to calculate the area of the rectangle, count or calculate the number of unit squares. Since there are five columns of unit squares and three rows, you can calculate the number of squares by multiplying 5 by 3 to get 15. Thus, the area of the rectangle is 15 square units.

31. B: To calculate the area of a rectangle, multiply its length by its width. For the given rectangle, multiply 2 by 3 to get 6. Thus, the area of the rectangle is 6 square units.

32. D: To calculate the area of a rectangle, multiply its length by its width. For the rectangular check, multiply 3 by 6 to get 18. Thus, the area of the check is 18 in^2.

33. A: Notice that the large rectangle is made of two smaller ones.

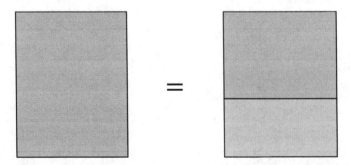

Therefore, the area of the large rectangle is equal to the sum of the areas of the smaller ones.

Large rectangle = Small rectangle + Small rectangle

To calculate the area of a rectangle, multiply its length by its width. The length of the large rectangle is 4, and its width is 3 + 2. Therefore, its area is 4 × (3 + 2). In the same way, we find that the areas of the two small rectangles are 4 × 3 and 4 × 2. Thus, the figure represents the equation below.

$$4 \times (3 + 2) = (4 \times 3) + (4 \times 2)$$

34. B: Break up the given figure into two rectangles. If necessary, find the length of any new sides.

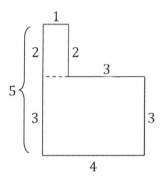

Now find the areas of the two rectangles by multiplying their lengths and their widths. Since the top rectangle is 1 unit by 2 units, its area is 2 square units. The bottom rectangle is 4 units by 3 units, so its area is 12 square units. Therefore, the area of the whole figure is 2 + 12 = 14 square units.

35. A: Break up the given figure into three rectangles. If necessary, find the lengths of any new sides.

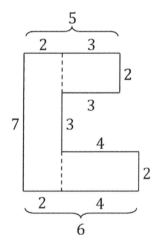

Now find the areas of the three rectangles by multiplying their length times their width. Since the top rectangle is 3 units by 2 units, its area is 6 square units. The left rectangle is 2 units by 7 units, so its area is 14 square units. The bottom rectangle is 4 units by 2 units, so its area is 8 square units. Therefore, the area of the whole figure is 6 + 14 + 8 = 28 square units.

36. A: First draw a picture of the rectangle.

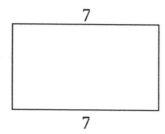

The perimeter of a rectangle is the sum of all of its side lengths. The perimeter of the rectangle is given as 22 units. Therefore, if we add (width + 7 + width + 7), the result will be 22.The only way this can happen is if the width is 4 units.

$$4 + 7 + 4 + 7 = 22$$

37. B: Carefully examine the three figures. Notice that all three sides of the equilateral triangle have the same lengths, all four sides of the square have the same lengths, and all five sides of the regular polygon have the same lengths. On the other hand, only the square has right angles. And only the triangle has three sides.

38. A: If a shape is partitioned (divided) into n parts of equal area, then the area of each part is $\frac{1}{n}$ of the whole. The given square is divided into 9 parts with equal areas, and one part is shaded. Therefore, the shaded area is $\frac{1}{9}$ of the total area.

Science

1. A: Organisms that are related tend to have similar traits. One way that scientists can tell whether organisms are related is to determine what traits they share. If the two islands have different terrains and climates, it's unlikely that the birds independently evolved similar traits by parallel evolution, and although it's *possible* that the similarities are coincidental, if the birds have many similar traits, this explanation is unlikely.

2. A: Organisms' traits change over time in response to the environment. If the main food available on the dry island is hard-shelled seeds, the birds are likely to develop traits that will better help them eat these seeds. The traits listed in the other choices are possible traits that the birds could develop, but there is nothing about the dry island that would make birds there more likely to develop those traits than the birds on the wet island.

3. C: *Inheritance* is the phenomenon of organisms having traits passed down from their parents. *Adaptation* refers to an organism or a group of organisms changing to be a better fit to their environment. *Diversity* refers to the existence of organisms or objects with many different traits and characteristics. *Variation* refers to differences among organisms or other objects.

4. C: If there are multiple forces acting on an object, the object will start moving unless the forces add up to zero. For two forces to add to zero, they have to be of the same size *and* be moving in opposite directions. It is therefore necessary to know the size of the forces and their direction to know whether or not the object will start moving.

5. D: The force between two magnets is larger if the magnets are stronger or closer together. The orientation of the magnets can also affect the strength of the magnets; the force between two bar magnets pointed with their ends toward each other, for instance, will be greater than the force between two bar magnets arranged in parallel at the same distance. The altitude above the Earth's surface will not affect the strength of the force between the magnets.

6. D: A force acting on a moving object can change its speed or direction. The effect depends on the direction of the force: if the force acts in the same direction as the object's motion, it will speed the object up; if the force acts in the opposite direction, it will slow the object down; and if it's acting at an angle to its motion, it will change the object's direction (and possibly also speed up the object or slow it down, if the force is not directly perpendicular to the object's motion).

7. B: During the summer, the days are longer and the nights are shorter, coming to an extreme at the summer solstice in late June (in the northern hemisphere; in the southern hemisphere, it's in late December). The days then get shorter during the fall, are shortest during the winter, and are at their very shortest on the winter solstice in late December (in the northern hemisphere; in the southern hemisphere, it's in late June).

8. A: It's important when taking measurements to have appropriate *control variables*—variables that don't change, so the only changes are in the particular phenomena that are being measured. Because the length of the day varies by the day of the year, in order to compare the lengths of the day in different cities, it's important to take those measurements on the same day of the year. There is no reason to use different clocks to measure the time of sunrise and sunset, and throwing out data that don't fit the expected results is very bad scientific practice because it will bias the data toward the experimenters' expectations.

9. B: The frogs in the polluted stream weigh less, which supports the statement that the pollution is stunting the growth of the frogs there. It's certainly possible that the pollution is also killing frogs in the polluted stream, but the data do not directly support that; the ecologist only measured the weight of the frogs, not the number of them.

10. C: To find an average, it's necessary to add together many measurements and divide by the number of them. All of the other methods mentioned are arbitrary and are not good ways of finding averages.

11. C: A *reversible* change is a change that can be easily changed back by reversing the process. Melting ice is reversible; the ice can be refrozen by subjecting it to temperatures below the freezing point of water. The other processes described are not reversible; there is no simple way to "unburn" paper, "uncook" meat, or "unshatter" a rock.

12. D: Degrees Celsius are used to measure temperature. The temperature at which water freezes is 0 degrees Celsius; water boils at 100 degrees Celsius. Length is measured in units such as meters or inches, and weight is measured in units such as pounds. There are no simple common units for hardness, although there are some relative scales it can be compared against, such as the Mohs scale used to characterize the hardness of rocks.

13.B: The bar corresponding to the month of March comes just short of the horizontal line that, according to the scale on the left, represents 3 inches of rain. So the amount of rain that month is a little less than 3 inches, or approximately 2.9 inches of rain.

14. C: The bar corresponding to the month of July is the shortest, so this is the month during which the least rain fell.

15. A: *Climate* refers to the variation in the weather over time and in different areas. *Ecology* describes the relationship between organisms and their environment; *precipitation* is the falling of water from the sky as rain, snow, or hail; and *prediction* is a guess or induction about what will happen in the future.

16. C: The plant treated with chemical #3 has the largest height, which suggests that this chemical may have been most beneficial for the plant growth. In fact, all the other plants are shorter than the plant that was untreated, suggesting that these chemicals may have actually been harmful for the plant's growth.

17. B: Although the data suggest that chemical #3 *may* be beneficial for the plant's growth, if the student only tested it with one plant, it could be that that particular plant just happened to be unusually tall and that the growth had nothing to do with the chemical. To make sure it was the chemical that was responsible, it would be best to do further trials using different plants. Doing more trials with different chemicals may find *other* chemicals that may be beneficial for the plant's growth, but it would not make more certain the results of the trials with *these* chemicals.

18. A: To check whether a particular change or treatment affects the results of an experiment, it's helpful to have one experimental subject left unchanged or untreated to compare to. This is the purpose of the plant without the chemical added. This unchanged or untreated subject is called an experimental *control*.

19. D: The student's results seem to show that the height of the plants is affected by the chemicals added to them. This suggests that an organism's traits can be affected by its environment. The other choices are true statements, but they are not directly supported by the student's data.

20. D: Sound is an example of a *wave*, carried by the vibration of the particles of the air.

21. B: Sound is a phenomenon associated with vibration of the particles of the air, and a sound can be caused by vibrations; the sound of a piano, for example, is caused by the vibration of the strings inside the piano, and the sound of your voice is caused by vibration of your vocal cords. Conversely, just as sound can be created by the vibration of an object, it can also cause objects nearby to vibrate.

22. D: If flooding is a problem in Harborton, some places are safer to build houses than others. Locations near riverbanks are not good places because rivers are likely to overflow their banks in a flood; canyons are also particularly dangerous in floods because they channel water through them. Hillsides may wash away in a flood, and a house built on a hillside might be in danger of sliding downhill. Of the listed sites, the safest is a rocky hilltop; the water will tend to flow downhill and away from the house, and the rocky ground will not wash away.

23. B: Lightning rods work because they conduct electricity safely into the ground, preventing it from damaging the rest of the house. As the highest points on a house, lightning rods are most likely to be hit by the lightning, and they are connected to the ground by conductive wires that channel the electrical energy from the lightning safely away from the house.

24. A: The safest place to be in a lightning storm is in an enclosed building, especially one protected by a lightning rod or another means to channel the lightning away. (Even indoors, you should stay away from exposed pipes or wiring or anything else that might conduct electricity from outside.) Lightning tends to hit the tallest objects in the area, so it's not safe to be in flat, open fields or in large bodies of water; it's also not safe to be directly under a tree because if the lightning hits the tree, you will probably be affected. If you're stuck outside in a lightning storm and can't reach a safe

building, the best thing to do is avoid open areas, do not get too close to trees or other tall objects, and crouch down and cover your ears.

25. B: Organisms that aren't around anymore, such as dinosaurs and wooly mammoths, are said to be *extinct. Evolved* just means that the organism changed over time, *symbiotic* refers to organisms that live together in a beneficial relationship, and *prehistoric* means before people started writing things down. Many organisms that lived in far prehistoric times are extinct, but there are other species that were around in prehistoric times and are still around today.

26. B: The petrified remains of ancient organisms are known as *fossils*; they form as the organic tissues of the organism decay and are replaced by deposited minerals. *Faults* and *geodes* are geologic features, and *vestigial* refers to a feature of an organism that serves little or no current purpose but is left over from a feature that served a purpose in the past.

27. C: Dinosaurs lived millions of years ago. More precisely, the first dinosaurs developed about 230 million years ago, and the last dinosaurs (excluding birds) died out about 66 million years ago.

28. A: The ball appears to show a pattern, passing in front of him every 12 minutes. He would therefore expect it to pass in front of him again 12 minutes after the last time; 36 minutes plus 12 minutes is 48 minutes.

29. C: Whenever an object's speed or direction is changing, there is a force acting on the object. If the ball is moving in a circle, its direction is changing, so there must be a force acting on it. The fact that the ball is moving does not mean by itself that there is a force acting on it; an object can be in motion without a force acting on it, but it will move in a straight line with a constant speed.

30. D: A *thermometer* is used to measure temperature. A *barometer* is used to measure pressure, and *centimeters* and *kilometers* are not instruments at all, but units of length.

Social Studies

1. C: Only Australia is entirely in the Southern Hemisphere. Parts of Africa and South America are in the Southern Hemisphere, but the continents are split between the two hemispheres. No part of Europe reaches into the Southern Hemisphere.

2. A: A peninsula is defined as a landform that is surrounded by water on three sides. An isthmus is a landform surrounded by water on two sides. A cliff is a landform overlooking water. An island is a landform completely surrounded by water.

3. B: Prior to the American Revolution and the founding of the United States, the states were known as colonies under Great Britain. The states were never officially known as territories, regions, or villages.

4. C: The legislative branch is responsible for making laws. The executive branch, or the president, is responsible for signing laws. The judicial branch is responsible for upholding laws. There is no federal branch of government; the word *federal* describes the type of government in the United States.

5. D: The Declaration of Independence announced that the American people no longer considered themselves part of Great Britain. The Bill of Rights represents the first 10 amendments to the US Constitution. The US Constitution is the founding document that laid out how the new government

would function. The Gettysburg Address is a speech that Abraham Lincoln gave after the deadly Battle of Gettysburg during the Civil War.

6. A: Tundra is a far northern landform known primarily for small plant life. Due to extreme cold, larger plants cannot grow there. A valley is a U-shaped or V-shaped landform that sits between large hills or mountains. It is not exclusive to far northern climates. A steppe is a wide grassland that may develop in any climate. A canyon is a deep landform that has developed from the erosion caused by water.

7. D: The so-called tea party, in which the American colonists dumped tea into the harbor, occurred in the city of Boston. It did not occur in New York, Yorktown, or Concord.

8. D: The number 3 identifies the continent of Africa. South America is identified by the number 2, and Asia is identified by the number 4. Europe is not identified by a number on the map.

9. B: Australia is not identified by a number at all. North American is identified by the number 1, Africa by the number 3, and Asia by the number 4.

10. D: A map is a flat representation of a round globe, so the Pacific Ocean exists both on the western shores of North and South America and on the eastern shores of Asia and Australia. As a result, the Pacific Ocean on the map above is represented by two letters: A and D. The Atlantic Ocean is represented only by the letter B. The Indian Ocean is represented by the letter C. The Arctic Ocean is not represented by any letter.

11. A: Each state sends two senators to Congress. The other answer choices indicate too many senators.

12. B: Each senator serves a single term of 6 years. Answer choice J is too low for any senatorial term. And, choices L and M are too high for a single senatorial term.

13. C: The number of representatives that each state sends to the House of Representatives is determined by the population of the state (as divided into districts). The number is not determined by a coin toss, the number of counties, or the size of the capital city.

14. B: A forest, a river, and coal are all natural resources because they exist in nature without any influence from human beings. A city, however, is not a natural resource because it is man-made.

15. D: An entrepreneur is someone who starts a business. Entrepreneurs may also run for public office and purchase stock in the stock market, but these activities are not exclusive to entrepreneurs. Additionally, an entrepreneur may run a restaurant, but a restaurant is not the only kind of business that defines an entrepreneur.

16. A: John Adams served as vice president to George Washington and later became the second president, after Washington. Thomas Jefferson, James Madison, and Abraham Lincoln did not serve as vice president under George Washington.

17. B: The judicial branch is responsible for applying the US Constitution to the interpretation of the laws and determining whether or not the laws meet the requirements of the US Constitution. The executive branch signs the laws. The legislative branch makes the laws. There is no federal branch of the government.

18. B: The word *currency* is another word to describe money. Money might be in circulation, but this describes the activities of money and not money itself. Money might also be exchanged, but

again this is an activity that applies to money. A tax is a type of charge used to support the government. It usually requires money, but once more, *tax* is not another word for money.

19. D: Fresh water is a need as every human being needs fresh water to survive. A candy bar, a dishwasher, and a new car would all be considered wants instead of needs.

20. D: To barter is to exchange one good or service for another. In this case, Kristina is exchanging her work of cleaning the studio for classes at the studio. Richard is mowing the lawn for free, so no exchange takes place. Jillian is saving money, so she is not planning to barter but rather to spend. In the same way, Mickey is charging for the lemonade and therefore receiving money for it.

21. C: Minot is directly east of Williston, so it is necessary to travel east. Minot is not north, south, or west of Williston.

22. B: From Minot, the first city directly south is Bismarck. From there, the first city directly west is Dickinson, so K is the correct answer. Answer choice J ignores the second set of directions (to travel west). Answer choice L goes east instead of west. Answer choice M goes east and then north.

23. B: No mountain is shown in the map of North Dakota. However, Lake Sakakawea, Theodore Roosevelt National Park, and the Missouri River and the Red River of the North are shown on the map.

24. A: The executive branch, in the form of the president, has the power of veto. The power of veto is not provided to the judicial or legislative branches, and there is no federal branch of government.

25. A: A country experiencing a drought will likely have to bring in, or import, food from countries around it. The doctor visiting another country to treat patients is neither importing nor exporting. The business owner could arguably be exporting the products to other states, but the business owner is not importing. The car manufacturer is simply making a local purchase and is neither importing nor exporting.

26. B: The country selling its silver to other countries is exporting that silver. The artist is donating a work but is neither importing nor exporting. The celebrity might be importing, if the gown is coming from a designer in another country; the celebrity is definitely not exporting. The boy is bartering his lunch; he is not importing or exporting.

27. D: Marla is providing the only example of producing by making cakes that she sells for weddings. Sallie, Donald, and Caroline might all be described as consumers, instead of producers.

28. C: Abraham Lincoln was president during the Civil War. Thomas Jefferson was president about 60 years before this (and was deceased long before the war occurred). Ulysses S. Grant was a general during the Civil War but did not become president until 4 years after the war had ended. Andrew Johnson was Lincoln's vice president and became president after Lincoln was assassinated and therefore after the Civil War.

29. B: A house painter is human being who provides a service and is thus a human resource. A computer program, a ballpoint pen, and a silver dollar are all nonhuman resources.

30. C: Florida was not one of the original Thirteen Colonies (later the original states) and was occupied by the Spanish until the early 19th century. New Hampshire, Massachusetts, and New York were all among the original states.

Vocabulary

1. B: something helpful

2. C: skill

3. D: very old

4. A: victory

5. D: weak

6. A: stop for a short time

7. C: empty

8. D: sleepy

9. B: far away

10. B: strange

11. C: stiff

12. B: not deep

13. C: hold

14. A: fall apart

15. A: think about

16. A: fast

17. C: wetness

18. D: watch

19. C: hard to find

20. D: maybe

21. B: sure

22. A: feel sadness about

23. C: very angry

24. B: give an answer

25. A: take place

26. D: sea

27. B: huge

28. C: bright

29. D: buy

Spelling

1. *gras* – this should be *grass*

2. *follo* – this should be *follow*

3. *deap* – this should be *deep*

4. *herry* – this should be *hairy*

5. *deel* – this should be *deal*

6. *berst* – this should be *burst*

7. toogether – this should be together

8. sumthing – this should be something

9. questun – this should be question

10. *boddle* – this should be *bottle*

11. *finul* – this should be *final*

12. wheather – this should be weather (or whether)

13. *restle* – this should be *wrestle*

14. tinsul – this should be tinsel

15. *arange* – this should be *arrange*

16. obzerve – this should be observe

17. *piramid* – this should be *pyramid*

18. *falt* – this should be *fault*

19. *sheeth* – this should be *sheath*

20. *suport* – this should be *support*

21. Wensday – this should be Wednesday

22. mischievious – this should be mischievous

23. thourully – this should be thoroughly

24. fernish – this should be furnish

Capitalization

1. NO MISTAKES

2. C: should be *to say, Mom*

3. A: should be Cheaper by the Dozen

4. C: should be Chicago, Illinois

5. A: should be Is Doctor Jones

6. A: should be *Be careful,*

7. B: should be a reporter interviewed

8. C: should be Yellowstone National Park.

9. B: should be Chairman of the

10. A: should be Muslims believe in Allah

11. C: should be company called Microsoft.

12. A: should be During World War II,

13. B: should be *New Year's Day*

14. B: should be *Reverend*

15. C: should be without Italian dressing.

16. B: should be You Should Exercise

17. B: should be during a blizzard

18. B: should be *New York Times*

19. B: should be *of the*

20. C: should be *Officer Smith*

Punctuation

1. A: Boise Idaho is should be Boise, Idaho is

2. B: to have snacks before supper, should be to have snacks before supper,"

3. C: usually get here" should be usually get here?"

4. A: Sir, Pedro exclaimed, should be "Sir," Pedro exclaimed,

5. B: is Paris which has over should be is Paris, which has over

6. C: Molly asked? should be Molly asked.

7. B: said Mr. Brown "you need should be said Mr. Brown, "you need

8. A: Des, Moines is should be Des Moines is

9. A: Dad said, "Lets go should be Dad said, "Let's go

10. D: NO MISTAKES

11. C: time it is. should be time it is

12. A: Ms. Ramirez said should be Ms. Ramirez said,

13. C: a few minutes? should be a few minutes.

14. C: Grandpa going to get here." should be Grandpa going to get here?"

15. B: if I were you", should be if I were you,"

16. A: The days of the week are, should be The days of the week are

17. C: time try again. should be time, try again.

18. A: "Stop this instant." should be "Stop this instant!"

19. B: to Deepak should be to Deepak,

20. C: I'm going you're going, should be I'm going, you're going,

How to Overcome Test Anxiety

Just the thought of taking a test is enough to make most people a little nervous. A test is an important event that can have a long-term impact on your future, so it's important to take it seriously and it's natural to feel anxious about performing well. But just because anxiety is normal, that doesn't mean that it's helpful in test taking, or that you should simply accept it as part of your life. Anxiety can have a variety of effects. These effects can be mild, like making you feel slightly nervous, or severe, like blocking your ability to focus or remember even a simple detail.

If you experience test anxiety—whether severe or mild—it's important to know how to beat it. To discover this, first you need to understand what causes test anxiety.

Causes of Test Anxiety

While we often think of anxiety as an uncontrollable emotional state, it can actually be caused by simple, practical things. One of the most common causes of test anxiety is that a person does not feel adequately prepared for their test. This feeling can be the result of many different issues such as poor study habits or lack of organization, but the most common culprit is time management. Starting to study too late, failing to organize your study time to cover all of the material, or being distracted while you study will mean that you're not well prepared for the test. This may lead to cramming the night before, which will cause you to be physically and mentally exhausted for the test. Poor time management also contributes to feelings of stress, fear, and hopelessness as you realize you are not well prepared but don't know what to do about it.

Other times, test anxiety is not related to your preparation for the test but comes from unresolved fear. This may be a past failure on a test, or poor performance on tests in general. It may come from comparing yourself to others who seem to be performing better or from the stress of living up to expectations. Anxiety may be driven by fears of the future—how failure on this test would affect your educational and career goals. These fears are often completely irrational, but they can still negatively impact your test performance.

Elements of Test Anxiety

As mentioned earlier, test anxiety is considered to be an emotional state, but it has physical and mental components as well. Sometimes you may not even realize that you are suffering from test anxiety until you notice the physical symptoms. These can include trembling hands, rapid heartbeat, sweating, nausea, and tense muscles. Extreme anxiety may lead to fainting or vomiting. Obviously, any of these symptoms can have a negative impact on testing. It is important to recognize them as soon as they begin to occur so that you can address the problem before it damages your performance.

The mental components of test anxiety include trouble focusing and inability to remember learned information. During a test, your mind is on high alert, which can help you recall information and stay focused for an extended period of time. However, anxiety interferes with your mind's natural processes, causing you to blank out, even on the questions you know well. The strain of testing during anxiety makes it difficult to stay focused, especially on a test that may take several hours. Extreme anxiety can take a huge mental toll, making it difficult not only to recall test information but even to understand the test questions or pull your thoughts together.

Effects of Test Anxiety

Test anxiety is like a disease—if left untreated, it will get progressively worse. Anxiety leads to poor performance, and this reinforces the feelings of fear and failure, which in turn lead to poor performances on subsequent tests. It can grow from a mild nervousness to a crippling condition. If allowed to progress, test anxiety can have a big impact on your schooling, and consequently on your future.

Test anxiety can spread to other parts of your life. Anxiety on tests can become anxiety in any stressful situation, and blanking on a test can turn into panicking in a job situation. But fortunately, you don't have to let anxiety rule your testing and determine your grades. There are a number of relatively simple steps you can take to move past anxiety and function normally on a test and in the rest of life.

Physical Steps for Beating Test Anxiety

While test anxiety is a serious problem, the good news is that it can be overcome. It doesn't have to control your ability to think and remember information. While it may take time, you can begin taking steps today to beat anxiety.

Just as your first hint that you may be struggling with anxiety comes from the physical symptoms, the first step to treating it is also physical. Rest is crucial for having a clear, strong mind. If you are tired, it is much easier to give in to anxiety. But if you establish good sleep habits, your body and mind will be ready to perform optimally, without the strain of exhaustion. Additionally, sleeping well helps you to retain information better, so you're more likely to recall the answers when you see the test questions.

Getting good sleep means more than going to bed on time. It's important to allow your brain time to relax. Take study breaks from time to time so it doesn't get overworked, and don't study right before bed. Take time to rest your mind before trying to rest your body, or you may find it difficult to fall asleep.

Along with sleep, other aspects of physical health are important in preparing for a test. Good nutrition is vital for good brain function. Sugary foods and drinks may give a burst of energy but this burst is followed by a crash, both physically and emotionally. Instead, fuel your body with protein and vitamin-rich foods.

Also, drink plenty of water. Dehydration can lead to headaches and exhaustion, especially if your brain is already under stress from the rigors of the test. Particularly if your test is a long one, drink water during the breaks. And if possible, take an energy-boosting snack to eat between sections.

Along with sleep and diet, a third important part of physical health is exercise. Maintaining a steady workout schedule is helpful, but even taking 5-minute study breaks to walk can help get your blood pumping faster and clear your head. Exercise also releases endorphins, which contribute to a positive feeling and can help combat test anxiety.

When you nurture your physical health, you are also contributing to your mental health. If your body is healthy, your mind is much more likely to be healthy as well. So take time to rest, nourish your body with healthy food and water, and get moving as much as possible. Taking these physical steps will make you stronger and more able to take the mental steps necessary to overcome test anxiety.

Mental Steps for Beating Test Anxiety

Working on the mental side of test anxiety can be more challenging, but as with the physical side, there are clear steps you can take to overcome it. As mentioned earlier, test anxiety often stems from lack of preparation, so the obvious solution is to prepare for the test. Effective studying may be the most important weapon you have for beating test anxiety, but you can and should employ several other mental tools to combat fear.

First, boost your confidence by reminding yourself of past success—tests or projects that you aced. If you're putting as much effort into preparing for this test as you did for those, there's no reason you should expect to fail here. Work hard to prepare; then trust your preparation.

Second, surround yourself with encouraging people. It can be helpful to find a study group, but be sure that the people you're around will encourage a positive attitude. If you spend time with others who are anxious or cynical, this will only contribute to your own anxiety. Look for others who are motivated to study hard from a desire to succeed, not from a fear of failure.

Third, reward yourself. A test is physically and mentally tiring, even without anxiety, and it can be helpful to have something to look forward to. Plan an activity following the test, regardless of the outcome, such as going to a movie or getting ice cream.

When you are taking the test, if you find yourself beginning to feel anxious, remind yourself that you know the material. Visualize successfully completing the test. Then take a few deep, relaxing breaths and return to it. Work through the questions carefully but with confidence, knowing that you are capable of succeeding.

Developing a healthy mental approach to test taking will also aid in other areas of life. Test anxiety affects more than just the actual test—it can be damaging to your mental health and even contribute to depression. It's important to beat test anxiety before it becomes a problem for more than testing.

Study Strategy

Being prepared for the test is necessary to combat anxiety, but what does being prepared look like? You may study for hours on end and still not feel prepared. What you need is a strategy for test prep. The next few pages outline our recommended steps to help you plan out and conquer the challenge of preparation.

STEP 1: SCOPE OUT THE TEST

Learn everything you can about the format (multiple choice, essay, etc.) and what will be on the test. Gather any study materials, course outlines, or sample exams that may be available. Not only will this help you to prepare, but knowing what to expect can help to alleviate test anxiety.

STEP 2: MAP OUT THE MATERIAL

Look through the textbook or study guide and make note of how many chapters or sections it has. Then divide these over the time you have. For example, if a book has 15 chapters and you have five days to study, you need to cover three chapters each day. Even better, if you have the time, leave an extra day at the end for overall review after you have gone through the material in depth.

If time is limited, you may need to prioritize the material. Look through it and make note of which sections you think you already have a good grasp on, and which need review. While you are studying, skim quickly through the familiar sections and take more time on the challenging parts.

Write out your plan so you don't get lost as you go. Having a written plan also helps you feel more in control of the study, so anxiety is less likely to arise from feeling overwhelmed at the amount to cover.

STEP 3: GATHER YOUR TOOLS

Decide what study method works best for you. Do you prefer to highlight in the book as you study and then go back over the highlighted portions? Or do you type out notes of the important information? Or is it helpful to make flashcards that you can carry with you? Assemble the pens, index cards, highlighters, post-it notes, and any other materials you may need so you won't be distracted by getting up to find things while you study.

If you're having a hard time retaining the information or organizing your notes, experiment with different methods. For example, try color-coding by subject with colored pens, highlighters, or post-it notes. If you learn better by hearing, try recording yourself reading your notes so you can listen while in the car, working out, or simply sitting at your desk. Ask a friend to quiz you from your flashcards, or try teaching someone the material to solidify it in your mind.

STEP 4: CREATE YOUR ENVIRONMENT

It's important to avoid distractions while you study. This includes both the obvious distractions like visitors and the subtle distractions like an uncomfortable chair (or a too-comfortable couch that makes you want to fall asleep). Set up the best study environment possible: good lighting and a comfortable work area. If background music helps you focus, you may want to turn it on, but otherwise keep the room quiet. If you are using a computer to take notes, be sure you don't have any other windows open, especially applications like social media, games, or anything else that could distract you. Silence your phone and turn off notifications. Be sure to keep water close by so you stay hydrated while you study (but avoid unhealthy drinks and snacks).

Also, take into account the best time of day to study. Are you freshest first thing in the morning? Try to set aside some time then to work through the material. Is your mind clearer in the afternoon or evening? Schedule your study session then. Another method is to study at the same time of day that you will take the test, so that your brain gets used to working on the material at that time and will be ready to focus at test time.

STEP 5: STUDY!

Once you have done all the study preparation, it's time to settle into the actual studying. Sit down, take a few moments to settle your mind so you can focus, and begin to follow your study plan. Don't give in to distractions or let yourself procrastinate. This is your time to prepare so you'll be ready to fearlessly approach the test. Make the most of the time and stay focused.

Of course, you don't want to burn out. If you study too long you may find that you're not retaining the information very well. Take regular study breaks. For example, taking five minutes out of every hour to walk briskly, breathing deeply and swinging your arms, can help your mind stay fresh.

As you get to the end of each chapter or section, it's a good idea to do a quick review. Remind yourself of what you learned and work on any difficult parts. When you feel that you've mastered the material, move on to the next part. At the end of your study session, briefly skim through your notes again.

But while review is helpful, cramming last minute is NOT. If at all possible, work ahead so that you won't need to fit all your study into the last day. Cramming overloads your brain with more information than it can process and retain, and your tired mind may struggle to recall even previously learned information when it is overwhelmed with last-minute study. Also, the urgent nature of cramming and the stress placed on your brain contribute to anxiety. You'll be more likely to go to the test feeling unprepared and having trouble thinking clearly.

So don't cram, and don't stay up late before the test, even just to review your notes at a leisurely pace. Your brain needs rest more than it needs to go over the information again. In fact, plan to finish your studies by noon or early afternoon the day before the test. Give your brain the rest of the day to relax or focus on other things, and get a good night's sleep. Then you will be fresh for the test and better able to recall what you've studied.

STEP 6: TAKE A PRACTICE TEST

Many courses offer sample tests, either online or in the study materials. This is an excellent resource to check whether you have mastered the material, as well as to prepare for the test format and environment.

Check the test format ahead of time: the number of questions, the type (multiple choice, free response, etc.), and the time limit. Then create a plan for working through them. For example, if you have 30 minutes to take a 60-question test, your limit is 30 seconds per question. Spend less time on the questions you know well so that you can take more time on the difficult ones.

If you have time to take several practice tests, take the first one open book, with no time limit. Work through the questions at your own pace and make sure you fully understand them. Gradually work up to taking a test under test conditions: sit at a desk with all study materials put away and set a timer. Pace yourself to make sure you finish the test with time to spare and go back to check your answers if you have time.

After each test, check your answers. On the questions you missed, be sure you understand why you missed them. Did you misread the question (tests can use tricky wording)? Did you forget the information? Or was it something you hadn't learned? Go back and study any shaky areas that the practice tests reveal.

Taking these tests not only helps with your grade, but also aids in combating test anxiety. If you're already used to the test conditions, you're less likely to worry about it, and working through tests until you're scoring well gives you a confidence boost. Go through the practice tests until you feel comfortable, and then you can go into the test knowing that you're ready for it.

Test Tips

On test day, you should be confident, knowing that you've prepared well and are ready to answer the questions. But aside from preparation, there are several test day strategies you can employ to maximize your performance.

First, as stated before, get a good night's sleep the night before the test (and for several nights before that, if possible). Go into the test with a fresh, alert mind rather than staying up late to study.

Try not to change too much about your normal routine on the day of the test. It's important to eat a nutritious breakfast, but if you normally don't eat breakfast at all, consider eating just a protein bar. If you're a coffee drinker, go ahead and have your normal coffee. Just make sure you time it so that the caffeine doesn't wear off right in the middle of your test. Avoid sugary beverages, and drink enough water to stay hydrated but not so much that you need a restroom break 10 minutes into the test. If your test isn't first thing in the morning, consider going for a walk or doing a light workout before the test to get your blood flowing.

Allow yourself enough time to get ready, and leave for the test with plenty of time to spare so you won't have the anxiety of scrambling to arrive in time. Another reason to be early is to select a good seat. It's helpful to sit away from doors and windows, which can be distracting. Find a good seat, get out your supplies, and settle your mind before the test begins.

When the test begins, start by going over the instructions carefully, even if you already know what to expect. Make sure you avoid any careless mistakes by following the directions.

Then begin working through the questions, pacing yourself as you've practiced. If you're not sure on an answer, don't spend too much time on it, and don't let it shake your confidence. Either skip it and come back later, or eliminate as many wrong answers as possible and guess among the remaining ones. Don't dwell on these questions as you continue—put them out of your mind and focus on what lies ahead.

Be sure to read all of the answer choices, even if you're sure the first one is the right answer. Sometimes you'll find a better one if you keep reading. But don't second-guess yourself if you do immediately know the answer. Your gut instinct is usually right. Don't let test anxiety rob you of the information you know.

If you have time at the end of the test (and if the test format allows), go back and review your answers. Be cautious about changing any, since your first instinct tends to be correct, but make sure you didn't misread any of the questions or accidentally mark the wrong answer choice. Look over any you skipped and make an educated guess.

At the end, leave the test feeling confident. You've done your best, so don't waste time worrying about your performance or wishing you could change anything. Instead, celebrate the successful completion of this test. And finally, use this test to learn how to deal with anxiety even better next time.

> **Review Video: Test Anxiety**
> Visit mometrix.com/academy and enter code: 100340

Important Qualification

Not all anxiety is created equal. If your test anxiety is causing major issues in your life beyond the classroom or testing center, or if you are experiencing troubling physical symptoms related to your anxiety, it may be a sign of a serious physiological or psychological condition. If this sounds like your situation, we strongly encourage you to seek professional help.

Additional Bonus Material

Due to our efforts to try to keep this book to a manageable length, we've created a link that will give you access to all of your additional bonus material:

mometrix.com/bonus948/itbsl9g3